Secrets &
Confidences

the complicated truth
about women's friendships

Secrets and Confidences
The Complicated Truth about Women's Friendships

Published by Seal Press
An Imprint of Avalon Publishing Group, Incorporated
1400 65th Street, Suite 250
AVALON Emeryville, CA 94608
publishing group incorporated

Library of Congress Cataloging-in-Publication Data
Eng, Karen.
  Secrets and confidences : the complicated truth about women's
relationships / By Karen Eng.
     p. cm.
  ISBN 1-58005-112-X (pbk.)
 1. Female friendship. 2. Female friendship—Anecdotes.
 3. Women—Psychology. 4. Interpersonal relations. I. Title.

HQ1206.E52 2004   302.3'4'082—dc22

ISBN 1-58005-112-X

9 8 7 6 5 4 3 2 1

Design by Amber Pirker
Printed in the United States of America by Worzalla
Distributed by Publishers Group West

for Anita

Contents

Introduction

Karen Eng

A few years ago, I went through a traumatic breakup with my best friend. Ours had been one of those impassioned, problematic girl-girl relationships that seem to thrive best in youth, when young women have time and the excess hormones to become completely absorbed in one another. Sparked at the tail end of our adolescence, evolving rapidly as we became young adults, this friendship was one I had hoped would remain central until we both got old.

But, as I learned the hard way, friendships between women, like all relationships, wax and wane. As the years passed, the passion wore off as the problems grew, and I finally decided, after much agonizing, to end it.

I wasn't quite prepared for how cataclysmic the experience would be. Deep down, I knew I was doing what was necessary for my own well-being, but there was little accepted wisdom about how to cope with my confusion and grief. Girlfriend breakups are the exception, not the rule. As such, they have no accepted script—as do, say, parental-rebellion or boyfriend-breakup speeches. Afterward, I obsessed about the way things had ended. Had I done the best I could for this friendship over the years? Did I handle the breakup right? If I had done the right thing, why did I feel so bereft?

If this had been a romantic relationship, answers would have been screaming at me from all directions. But because this was "only" a friend, prescriptions were vague and solace hard to come by. Women are supposed to discard a chain of men before they find Mr. Right, but we are supposed to accumulate meaningful female friendships, not jettison them. In a time when people accept the view that many, if not most, marriages founder, we still cling to the view that our friendships should somehow go on for life.

And sometimes they do. All this got me thinking about the other women in my life, many of whom have been around since girlhood. I count myself lucky to have the ability to make friends quickly and deeply, and many of my happiest hours have been in the company of women whose tastes and values and sense of humor complement mine. Where would I have been without my friends?

Recently, it's pretty much been seared into our consciousness by certain extremely popular television shows (and attendant constant commentary) that the public image of female friendships consists of shoe shopping, martini lunches, wedding-dress envy, fertility angst, and impending moves to Paris. As much as we love those shows, it's precisely because we know they aren't real. And we know what *is* real is infinitely more difficult—and more interesting.

Female friendships must be the most oversimplified, trivialized, underappreciated, and misunderstood of relationships. In direct conflict with women's own expectation of a lifelong, consistently intense bond with their girlfriends, society dictates that girlfriends come after children, spouses, parents, and siblings, roughly in that order. But to relegate friendships to fourth or fifth place is to seriously devalue them. Even before we've become adults and left our parents behind, friends are in the trenches with us on the front lines of childhood. Friends are who we explore the world with when we first venture out of the nest. When friends don't come easily, we long for them, look for them in books and movies. Our first best friend is the first person we come to love outside our immediate families—because we just do, not because we have to. She is our first ally, the first stranger in a parade of many we'll encounter in our lives who will mold and challenge our ideas of who we are, often in conflict with who our parents and society tell us we're supposed to be.

Friends at their best adore our quirks, indulge our sins, champion our successes, and downplay our faults, often more effortlessly than families and lovers do. On the other side of the coin, women have often unrealistically high—and unspoken—expectations of each other, a dynamic that seems to start on the playground as we form our alliances with and against other girls. From a young age, the edict against abandonment is but one of many tacit commandments:

Thou shalt accommodate your friend's needs at the expense of your own

Thou shalt reveal all thy innermost secrets

Thou shalt listen with support and never voice criticism

Thou shalt be there for your friend 24/7

Thou shalt not succeed where your friend has failed

These are the requirements for entry into a female alliance, and any breach is a serious betrayal.

Clearly these relationships are crucial as well as complex. Yet there's little in the way of formalizing or acknowledging them, much less legal or social sanction—no naming ceremony, no promise rings, no wedding, no anniversary parties, no marches or even civil unions. Celebrating friendship happens in the blandest of Hallmark-card terms; women's friendships are not taken seriously. Accordingly, when things go wrong, that too is not taken seriously, and the consequences can be devastating.

Sure enough, when I trolled the shelves for a book that might give me some much-needed insight after my big breakup, the few books about women's friendships I could find were either fluffy, gift-book volumes about how your best friend is always there for you—*if only,* I thought—or grim academic works analyzing the cruelty of schoolgirls. I couldn't stomach either.

I knew I could really only take comfort in a book that contained intimate, thoughtful tales of friendships like mine—with all the ecstasy, agony, and absurdity intact—written from the point of view of my peers. Such a book would show in vivid detail how and why women's bonds are so fascinating and funny and complex. It would be necessarily political, because friendships are the first place where we practice, or don't, what we preach, and usually where we're first called on our shortcomings. When I broached the idea of such a book with fellow writers, editors, and artists, they agreed heartily—and suddenly, I couldn't *not* put the idea into motion. It was in this spirit of enthusiasm and collaboration that we set out to produce a collection that begins to chart the unexplored territory of real friendships between real women.

I say "begins" because a book of twenty-three pieces can barely hope to scratch the surface. For every story included in this volume, there are a hundred waiting to be told. The friendships you will read about in this collection take place on university campuses, on beaches in Britain and Israel, in poor dwellings in Africa, suburban bedrooms and basements, urban playgrounds and schools. The stories are of bonds forged through girlhood, motherhood, artistic striving, and plain survival, across class, culture, race, geographical distance, and time.

So here's an inside view of the hope and elation we experience in our relationships, the craziness and unlikelihood of some of our bonds, as well as some of the inevitable disappointments and grief. I hope these stories get passed along as the gifts that they are, along the way offering insight, saying what's often left unsaid, and honoring the essence of being female and a friend.

Cowboys and Indians

Jennifer Maher

Sadie Fink was my first true love. We became friends in fifth-grade phonics group, both misdiagnosed as "slow" readers because, though we'd both been reading at a junior-high level since the age of nine, we couldn't pass a phonics test to save our lives. So, we were lumped in with a group of kids who not only couldn't pass phonics but who had never, not even once, read *Harriet the Spy*.

We had been eyeing each other warily before this moment, though. As when boy meets girl, there was lots of looking, locking eyes, and looking down again. I wasn't happy with my relationship at the time; neither was she. I hung out mostly with Tracey, a girl with whom I had little in common besides a history of Barbie melodrama and a shared love of sno-cones. Sadie was friends with Bridget, a sweet kid whose father, though Jewish, had an Irish fetish. He even started a jeans line called Bridget Girl with a shamrock on the label.

I saw their differences early on and predicted a breakup even before I was interested in Sadie. For one thing, Bridget was sporty and especially good at tetherball, whereas Sadie's first impulse (like mine) when a ball headed her way was to cover her head with a book. They were miles apart intellectually as well. Once I overheard Bridget complaining about a girl making fun of her for being Jewish. Sadie, also Jewish, advised her to take the most direct, confrontational approach:

"Get right in her face like this and shout, 'I'M A DAUGHTER OF DAVID, YOU DUMMY!'" she urged.

"David who?" Bridget asked.

"Oh, never mind," Sadie said, rubbing her forehead.

We all went to a private school as a result of a dying progressive-policy attempt to create a more level playing field in the public schools. "Busing," it was called, and it left parents like ours in the awkward position of having to live their politics. They'd claim they supported busing in principle, but that it wasn't right for us to have to take a long bus ride to a school where we had no "peers"—meaning other white children of liberal parents who drove Toyotas with Peace Now bumper stickers. The private-school market grew exponentially from such fears, and a makeshift school like ours, Woodcrest, presented itself as an option for the non-Catholic. It was more affordable than its uniform-wearing counterparts, but it wasn't cheap. It enrolled a variety of kids—from those whose parents were spending every last penny for them to attend (sometimes living in teeny apartments or with the grandparents) to those who got their homework assignments in advance to complete before the annual family trip to Aruba.

Sadie and I belonged to the former category. We weren't picked up in Jaguars by stay-at-home moms in tennis whites at 3:30. Rather, we stayed around until 5:45 or so, because that's when our mothers got off work. This meant we were free to run around on a nearly empty playground with our jacket hoods on our heads as makeshift capes or long princess hair, while some teenager getting paid to make sure we didn't get abducted finished her homework. The closer it got to five, the fewer of us there were: usually just Sadie and me, plus Jennifer Boles, whose mother was a cocktail waitress and whose father fixed pinball machines. And Summer, who moved in a higher social stratum than her late after-school pickup would lead one to believe. Her father was a minor rock star who didn't drop her off in the mornings until 10 A.M., when she'd climb out of their airbrushed van as if she were Stevie Nicks herself. We'd crowd the classroom window to watch her gorgeous father—in his fraying shirt and velvet pants—flip his hair, kiss her on the cheek, and hand her a Big Gulp and a doughnut before climbing back in and driving off to the recording studio.

Neither Sadie nor I had such glamour on our side. We were outcasts. Both of us lived with our single mothers, which added to this status, though not in the way you might think: This was the time of Studio 54—less about scarlet letters than scarlet-sequined tube tops. No, our chief problem was that we never quite looked "right" because we didn't have the money to style ourselves appropriately. First, there was the hair, which our mothers cut for us. At the height of Farrah hysteria, ours just wouldn't cooperate. Sadie's was dark, wavy, and beautiful, but resistant to the fixed style of "feathering." Mine was so thin and fine it just wouldn't do anything. I could sometimes force the sides into a wing shape by freezing my hair with my hand and then spraying it to death, but even then the bottom hung like yellow yarn strings on a wool beanie pompom.

Additionally, we were hopelessly out of fashion, and the harder we tried, the worse it was. While the rich girls wore gold S-chains with Italian horns, or #1 Kid charms, we had gold-plated ones from JC Penney. This seemed okay until one of us would be in the lunch line behind Michelle, or Tiffany, or Madison, who'd say, "Oooooh, pretty necklace," turning it this way and that, looking for the telltale 14K stamp. Finding none, they'd whisper to each other and roll their eyes. Instead of Lacoste shirts, we wore Le Tigre, a poor-kid fake brand that replaced the little blue alligator with a little blue tiger. Again, fine from a distance, deadly in the next-up-to-bat P.E. line.

We were both wearing Le Tigre shirts—mine purple, hers yellow—the day we officially bonded in phonics group. Our teacher, Grace, was an ex-hippie, which meant we began each day with a Pete Seeger or Joan Baez song. She put us in "learning clusters" based on our supposed abilities, rewarding students in the higher groups with more interesting assignments, like reading *The Hobbit*. Sadie and I formed a professional alliance early, filling in our other group members' workbook pages so we could then read our own books or draw. We already knew how to spell and read, but neither of us could master that phonics book. It was supposed to be about words, but somehow it scrambled everything up and made it look like math.

It was the "schwa" business that finally sent Sadie over the edge and initiated the friendship. We were taking turns answering phonics questions with Grace, while the kids in Group One got to practice writing their own short stories. Sadie was picking at a hangnail and sighing loudly. When her question in the workbook came up, Grace turned to her, saying, "Now, Sadie, this question is asking, 'What sound does a schwa make?'" No answer.

"Sadie, is there something that you don't understand about the schwa? Remember on page seventeen when we looked at the symbol in those other words? We can go back and look together as a group if you think it . . ."

"SCHWA!" Sadie shouted, throwing her arms back behind her like the first swimmer about to jump off the edge of the pool for a relay race.

"The SCHWA makes the SCHWA sound, OK? SCHWA! SCHWA-SCHWA-SCHWA-SCHWA! God."

Grace's face twitched, as if she had accidentally swallowed a gnat, but she recovered quickly, saying, "Sadie, I think you need some cool-down time, to think about how outbursts like that hurt the group."

Sadie quietly shut her notebook and got up, but not before her eyes met mine and we started laughing. Even after she was sitting with her back to me across the room, I could still see her shoulders shaking up and down silently, and I could not stop the heaving noises coming through my nose. Luckily, trying to hold back my laughter for so long resulted in a mild asthma attack, just in the nick of time. I was sent to the office for my inhaler rather than for interrupting "together learning time."

After that, we began spending every minute we could with each other, dropping our other friends unceremoniously and indulging in the private secret language and customs of love. We would try to wear the same colors to school and pretend it was an accident. Sadie's dad bought her a real gold Best Friend charm, a serious trend in those days. It was a heart with a kind of lightning-bolt crack down the middle, and you wore one half while your best friend wore the other. Our mothers became friends, sort of, sharing the occasional smoke or two and complaining about our bastard fathers before they took one or the other of us home from one or the other of our houses. People began calling us Starsky and Hutch.

The honeymoon lasted only until Halloween. The beginning of the end, I have come to believe, started with our school pumpkin-carving contest, though I couldn't have said this at the time. Mr. Berman, our social studies teacher, was the judge, and though parents could opt out altogether, my mother did her best to participate, aided by Sadie's mother, Jackie, and a pitcher of homemade margaritas.

The official directions specified that children were supposed to do the work on the pumpkins, adults helping only with the use of sharp objects. But as the night wore on and the drinks continued, we were summarily (if silently) excused. As far as I can remember, all I did that night was pull the pumpkin guts out and toss them in the garbage disposal.

My mother had recently acquired a new position at Walt Disney, which is where she got the idea for my pumpkin. Using wire and black silk, she constructed Mickey Mouse ears to be held onto the pumpkin's head with pushpins. Jackie carved the eyes and used Liquid Paper to make the whites of them. Through lack of time or poor planning, no one thought to paint the pumpkin white; though it looked passable, it also looked like Mickey had taken too many of those self-tanning pills you saw advertised in the back of *Cosmopolitan*.

Jackie was working on Sadie's pumpkin, a lopsided facsimile of Cher's head whose orange skin and taped-on Indian feathers made a bit more sense than a tan Mickey Mouse. As our mothers worked away, we sat at the table and drew pictures of horses, a growing obsession of Sadie's, and one I was getting tired of. The room she shared with her younger brother was separated by cinder block–and-pine bookshelves where she had painstakingly lined up over fifteen breeds of plastic horses in alphabetical order, and still, this was all she wanted to draw. I wanted to trace the photo of the stars of *Charlie's Angels* from the cover of *Time* but was reduced to negotiating with Sadie to at least let me make one of the horse manes feathered.

The next morning, with Halloween three days away, we carried our pumpkins into the auditorium. Although neither of us expected to win, we couldn't help but be shocked by the scene on the lunch benches. Our school went up to the seventh grade, and it was clear that the older kids' more-sophisticated imaginations had pushed their parents—this being Los Angeles, these were set designers and makeup artists in the "industry"—to create ever more sophisticated spectacles. There was a set of KISS pumpkins, complete with a motion-sensor tape loop of "Rock and Roll All Nite." Though the number of children passing it eventually wore out its batteries, the concept won out, and the display sat proudly on one of the prize tables. Next to it perched Shanni Singh's award-winning, spray-painted blue, many-armed Shiva perched on a huge butternut squash hand painted with illustrations from the Bhagavad Gita. The butternut cushion and Shiva's zucchini-constructed arms broke the pumpkin-only rule, but, Shanni's homeroom teacher offered, they were from India and were therefore confused. But the pièce de résistance, truly a wonder to behold, sat in the center of the last table, rising at least three feet higher than the rest of the pumpkins worshipping at its base. The grand-prize winner consisted of a lifelike sculpture in gray clay of a headless man riding a rearing horse (its naturalistic mane *not* feathered). Its painstakingly carved, nineteenth century–sleeved arm stuck out at a perfect forty-five-degree angle, a pumpkin resting elegantly on its outstretched palm.

Because it involved a horse, we had to visit it repeatedly. The smell of cafeteria food nauseated Sadie, so we could view it only in short bursts, but we did, over and over before the first class began, and again at recess and again after school. Sadie held her breath longer and longer, trying not to cry with envy.

Thoroughly crestfallen by five o'clock, we prepared to carry our naive pumpkins home. We were not going to tell our mothers that the white Winner! ribbons pinned to them were a pathetic appeasement put on all of the pumpkins, just like the Good Worker awards passed out to everyone except those who got Excellent Worker at the end of the school year. However, the end of October was a downright chilly sixty degrees by five, sending assorted working mothers into the auditorium to collect children normally hailed from the playground.

When my mother came to pick me up, she saw the Headless Horseman and gasped. She grabbed my jacket rather violently, rushing out before I could say goodbye to anyone. We drove straight to the McDonald's drive-through, where she let me get a pumpkin shake and a McGoblin figurine with no haggling on my part whatsoever. I was allowed to eat in front of the TV watching *Charlie's Angels*, something normally forbidden ("bimbettes," she called them), and dip my french fries into my shake, a habit she hated. Nothing really came of this at first, and it seemed to have little to do with Sadie and me. That is, until the "Social Studies in Three Dimensions" assignment a couple of months later. Perhaps high on his power as pumpkin-contest judge, Mr. Berman assigned us to make something in three dimensions representing some aspect of American history listed in the timeline at the front of our Harcourt-Brace *Introduction to Your Nation* textbook. It was specified, again, that children were to construct the model on their own, with only minimal help from their parents. But my mother was having none of it. Of course, she also left for work at 6:30 A.M. and didn't get home until 6:30 P.M. And then, suddenly, it was Sunday night and we had to come up with something, so we did the best we could with the limited materials available from the drugstore. On a piece of thick-backed construction paper, we hand-glued inch-tall plastic cowboys and Indians fighting around a fence, the lot of them—fence included!—purchased in one convenient ninety-nine-cent plastic bag. I colored in ground and arrows as best I could since we made the mistake of gluing on the figurines—blue cowboys shooting, red and orange Indians kneeling with tomahawks and headdresses like rooster combs—before I'd thought to trompe l'oeil the poster board itself.

It was the first time we had actually worked on anything together, except for the agonizing hours we spent on my long-division homework that I failed anyway since in England (where my mother is from) they multiplied in a singsong rhyme. I got busted for not "showing my work," which seemed absurd since I had memorized "seven sevens are forty-nine" and hence considered adding up the quantity on the side of the page redundant. This was different, though, because it didn't make me cry like math did. My mother showed an expertise with Elmer's I could hardly have imagined, considering her absolute lack of interest in coloring, drawing, or crafts of any kind. Toward the end of her fifth Virginia Slim, she got downright giddy and ripped some grass and leaves out of the front lawn to sprinkle on the cardboard as a final effect.

But my heart sank as we took it into the classroom and I saw the other, intricate mini-dioramas. In that class alone, five of the fathers had jobs in the animation department at Disney. After I caught my breath and put down our cardboard, plastic, and dirt—much of the grass had blown off during the walk from the parking lot—I saw, among other concoctions, the following lined up along a row of desks at the front of the room:

A twelve-inch-high adobe church with meticulously hand-molded Play-Doh tiles on its roof and a working bell that rang when you pulled a string cleverly hidden in a bonsai bush at the front.

A shoebox on its side with a teeny *Niña*, *Pinta*, and *Santa María*—with the historically accurate number of paper sails on each—resting between layers of hand-painted tissue-paper ocean that moved when you twisted two knobs at the side of the box.

Some sort of Indian village thing with orange-painted Barbies in hand-sewn burlap costumes, with a volcano in the back that let off a wisp of steam when you hit a button hidden under a tepee.

Sadie's project, like mine, appeared awful and amateurish in comparison, but for different reasons. She had, in fact, crafted hers in the formal sense of the term, in that she had made Play-Doh models of the Beatles getting off of one of her old Barbie airplanes. A picture of a crowd, cut out of one of her father's NASCAR magazines, was affixed beside the plane. She had even transformed one of her brother's action figures into a bobby, covering him in blue felt, giving him a twig for a nightstick, and sitting him on top of one of her plastic horses. It was clever, but totally flawed in its execution. You couldn't really tell one Beatle from another, and the boundary between their skin and their jackets was turning green from the Magic Marker she'd used to color their suits. But she got a B. I got a C-. The index card next to hers was filled with praise like "Great idea!! Glad to see you really making an effort!!!" Mine said, "This is a piece of cardboard with plastic toys glued onto it." Out of compassion, Sadie sneaked up on the index card to change my grade to a C+, which resulted in the two of us in the principal's office, questioned separately as if we were partners in a counterfeiting scheme—which I suppose in a way we were.

Sadie's mother was furious with her and could hardly look at me as she led Sadie to the car that night. My mother was called in later. She lost it with the principal, lighting up in the trophy-studded office and blowing smoke through her nose when she heard about the grade I (originally) received. She said something to the effect that she had neither the time nor the money to construct adobe houses or paper oceans, and it was supposed to be a child's project to begin with, and she knew goddamn well who those parents were and had actually seen them huddled over small pieces of clay and paper at the Disney commissary that very week. Besides which, even though she was English she knew bloody well the Cheyenne Indians didn't live anywhere near bloody volcanoes.

The grade didn't change. That didn't bother me as much as the change that seemed to take place in Sadie over the next couple of weeks. Summer's father, it turns out, went crazy for her piece; he thought it was the funniest and coolest thing ever. He *paid* for the damn thing, and there was a picture of Sadie handing it to him in the school newsletter. She was wearing, I should add, a brand-new sundress and Famolare shoes, courtesy of the family Sears card.

Sadie even got invited to spend the night at Summer's house. And she went. I was crushed. I wouldn't think of spending the night at someone else's house, or at least I wouldn't tell her if I did. For days I was regaled with descriptions of the décor (lots of Oriental carpets and fringed table lamps), the food (a casserole with potato chips on top, and even a splash of wine in a glass whose stem was designed to look like a dragon's tail), and the pets (a parakeet named Apple and two Chihuahuas named Pico and Sepulveda). All I could do was pout, which probably made me very unpleasant to be around, driving her further into the clutches of the in-crowd. She even started playing volleyball, which was as sure a sign we were headed for trouble as lipstick on the proverbial collar.

Not that we ever had a direct confrontation about this. Sadie never totally "dumped" me, as I think I offered her something that Summer's crowd couldn't: freedom to be her wavy-haired self; a chance not to worry every second about whether she was wearing or doing the right thing. We still occasionally had long giggling fits on the phone, and when it was just the two of us left on the playground at night, it felt like old times. But the notes we passed got shorter and shorter, and she didn't eat lunch with me anymore. Twice when I called her during the week her mother said she wasn't there, though she wouldn't tell me where she was. I took to riding my bike to her house and peeking around—for what, I'm not sure. I wanted to catch her in the act—tanning in the yard with one of the popular girls, say, or making up dances to ELO songs like we used to do on the curb. Instead I just scrabbled for the crumbs she threw me. I was, in fact, losing my first true love. If I'd asked in the right way, I'm sure she would have said, "It's not you, it's me," or "I need to see other people right now," or "I need my space."

Yet somehow she swung me an invite to the slumber birthday party of a popular girl, Hailey. I'm not sure whether it was because Sadie missed me, or felt sorry for me, or both. No matter what, I was determined to do this right. I was going to be accepted. I wore my one good pair of jeans, put on the Best Friend necklace (though Sadie didn't wear hers anymore; she said she had lost it), and borrowed my mother's rolling suitcase and my sister's Serious Camper sleeping bag. We went out to pizza and Hailey opened present after present, gifts that, had I received even one of them, I'd be shaking over. But her response to a new gold heart charm or another pair of Calvin Klein jeans was just a quick smile and a "Thanks, Mom," until she moved on to the next item. Her parents had a condominium with a hot tub and an answering machine and a huge TV that had these big red, green, and yellow lights on it, so the cast of *The Love Boat* looked even more glamorous than usual. There was mirrored wallpaper in the bathroom. We were allowed to sleep in our bathing suits. I was mesmerized.

As the evening wore on and all of us, high on sugar and lack of sleep, started talking about school and the teachers we hated so much we were going to look them up and crank-call them, I felt perfectly

11

comfortable stating my opinion: Mr. Berman was the most vile and, worst of all, the most unfair. I launched into the pumpkin-carving contest first, describing the humiliation Sadie and I went through over our pumpkins versus Paul Stinson's, he of the Headless Horseman and special effects–coordinator father. I talked about the social studies project and its underhanded nature, too. I described how unfair it was for a teacher to tell kids to work on something themselves and then reward those who obviously hadn't. It was an injustice and it needed to be stopped.

I must have been going at it for a while because, before I had the chance to notice, the room had gone quiet. Hailey's pumpkin, a model of Cinderella's carriage—with tiny hand-carved wooden mice and a Barbie shoe painted silver—had, in fact, won a prize. Probably one of the other girls was the proud owner of the adobe church with the hidden bell or the Columbus Discovers America shoebox. I was terrifically embarrassed, and when Sadie opened her mouth I was expecting a save of some sort. But the only person she was saving was herself.

"But, wait," she began quietly. "Your mom *did* do most of your social studies project. And she, like, made the pumpkin, too, just like my mom did. They just aren't, like, talented or anything. They just didn't do it good enough."

My stomach dropped. I couldn't think of a word to say.

The moment passed, thank god, when Hailey's mother arrived with a plate of Double Stuf Oreos. I tried to eat them, but they felt like crushed porcelain in my throat.

I slept on and off that night, and between awake and asleep a series of disconnected pictures flashed through my mind: tissue-paper oceans, our kitchen table with the pen marks on it, the horse Sadie would never get, my mother at a disco. Images rained down like loose grass blown onto poster board: dinner plates, phone cords, fathers. Sadie's ease with this situation felt like a punch in the stomach. Her betrayal was offhand, but profound. I feared a future I couldn't fit myself into. This world was made for those who did things good enough, or who were loved by the ones who did things good enough. Or for the ones who had neither talent nor the love of the talented, but were lucky enough to feel okay about this fact.

Mr. Berman, I thought, knew all of this, and he graded—our projects, our pumpkins, our parents—accordingly. I woke up with a start that night in a stranger's condominium. In my dream I had been trying to cover my head against a rain of plastic cowboys and Indians, their guns and tomahawks catching in my hair, their teeny bodies tensed upon my shoulders, crouched low and ready for a fight. I searched for Sadie in the shapes of the sleeping girls around me, but I couldn't find her anywhere.

Breaking Up with Smitty

Andi Zeisler

"[Friendships] are easy to get out of compared to love affairs, but they are not easy to get out of compared to, say, jail." —Fran Lebowitz

An article clipped from *The New York Times Magazine* arrived at my apartment one afternoon, in an envelope marked with my mother's return address. It was not accompanied by a note. The article, from their "How To" issue, a special affair featuring service articles of the intellectually insouciant kind, was titled "How to Dump a Friend."

"In high school," wrote author Lucinda Rosenfeld, "blowing off a friend was as easy as sitting at a different table in the cafeteria. . . . In the more passive-aggressive arena of adult life, the weeding process is typically accomplished via unreturned phone calls and the chronic cancellation of social engagements 45 minutes before they're due to take place. This is because, at heart, adults are huge wimps."

I know I was. I'd been trying to think of easy, painless ways to extricate myself from Smitty for months, and for months I had been foiled by intrusions both physical and logistical: I can't break up with her; she's about to have her baby. I can't break up with her; I'm going out of town tomorrow and don't have time. I can't break up with her; there are too many people at this party. I'd exhausted even my journal with anguished, wimpy hashings-over of these aborted endings. But I was finally gearing up for the finish. We had a lunch date planned, and just thinking about it made my chest seize with nervous, painful hiccups. I pictured us sitting over fancy salads dotted with walnuts and lumps of feta and tried to imagine how I would do it. "I've been thinking about this," I would start, "and it's become clear that this relationship is going nowhere. You make time for everyone in your life but me, and I resent it."

"What?" she would say, straining to hear me over the hip little bistro's sound system, her baby's fussy noises, the tinkling of forks and knives. "What are you talking about?" Then our dogs, tied up outside, would start to bark and lunge, the baby would burst into tears and require breastfeeding, and the waitress would come over to see if we needed more iced tea. The moment would be gone. "Nothing," I'd say. "Don't worry about it."

As usual, the way it ended was both nothing and everything like I thought it would be. She was late for our lunch date, so I called her house. "Oh," she said, after I mentioned that I was still sitting at my desk, waiting for her to come pick me up. "I completely forgot that we were supposed to have lunch. I can't come. I have food poisoning." This last was said with the breezy nonchalance of someone in the midst of a soothing mani-pedi, as opposed to doubled over in front of the toilet. "Well, maybe tomorrow," I said, "when you're feeling better." "Yes, tomorrow, definitely," she said. We hung up, and I opened a new file on my computer and started to write a letter.

Breaking Up with Smitty

It probably says a lot that Smitty and I were never supposed to meet.

We were set up in a case of mistaken identity too convoluted to go into, but the gist is that I needed some part-time work and she had some to offer. Once we realized that I wasn't who she thought I was, we both shrugged, and she hired me on the spot. I started doing grunt work for her small textile-design business that day, while she shuffled around the studio in her pajamas, drinking coffee, yelling at her dog, the phone constantly at her ear. There was something about her that I didn't trust. There was something about her that I didn't like. And there was something else, something that made me say I'd see her the next day, and immediately start looking forward to it.

Most of us can claim to have a "type," in the cutesy, pseudoscientific parlance of romance. Neurotics, musicians, neat freaks, sex maniacs: They aren't necessarily the people we should be with, or even particularly want to be with, but they are nevertheless the people we fall in with over and over. And so it goes with many friendships. I too have a type, at least when it comes to women. Though most of the friends I have aren't this type, the most memorable ones, for better or for worse, are. Some call her a drama queen; some, less diplomatically, call her a pain in the ass. Psychiatrists tell me she's a narcissistically disordered personality. Few, in any case, would argue that she's anything less than high, high maintenance. For me, she's always been the dangerous friend.

When you're young, the dangerous friend urges you to shoplift, strands you in the bad part of town when you have an argument, dogears the good parts of *Forever* and leaves it in your room where your mother is sure to spy it. She may be the person who first gets you drunk or engineers the loss of your virginity to some guy she knows. In the case of my dangerous friend, she also may have the impeccable timing to run away from home and land on your doorstep only minutes after you've dropped a tab of LSD, with the upshot being that you'll have an extremely psychedelic conversation with the several cops who subsequently visit your house.

But the dangerous friend isn't dangerous because she's daring, or precocious, or even reckless. She's dangerous because she makes you trust her against all logical judgment, makes you want to please her even if your own happiness is compromised, and imprints herself on your mind with disconcerting speed and force.

And that's exactly how it went with Smitty. It was as if, from the moment she opened the door to our mistaken interview, talking a mile a minute, she had chosen me. It was nothing so cosmic, of course—it was simply that Smitty, it quickly became clear to me, refused to separate her work from her friends, and by signing on as her employee, I'd also signed on to be her buddy.

Smitty's day began—and progressed and ended—with a succession of phone calls. Whether she was talking to the president of a company, her accountant, her current best friend, or her mother, the tone was one that combined mocking, bossing, teasing, and bullying. She was an artist, married and divorced by the age of twenty-eight, rowdy, with the curly-haired, wide-mouthed, slightly madcap aspect of a '40s comedienne—Judy Garland crossed with Carrie Bradshaw. Like the rest of my dangerous friends, she used the phone as a measure of her popularity and expected everyone else in the room to eavesdrop. Thus were friends and employees expected to become well versed in her life, her idiosyncrasies, and her sense of humor—scholars of Smittyology.

Occasionally, between phone calls, she would study me as I worked at a drafting table across the room and ask a probing, often inappropriate, personal question. It was hard to tell whether she was sincerely curious or whether she simply wanted to shock me into paying full attention to her. Regardless, almost immediately after clocking my reaction to such queries, she would take a dramatic conversational U-turn. "Are you a lesbian?" she once asked. "The day I met you I was sure you were. You have a lesbian vibe." Then, remarking of the skinny English pointer that spent the workday with his nose lodged alternately in the garbage can and in the vicinity of my crotch, she said, "I got him at the shelter on the day after my grandmother died in my arms."

Breaking Up with Smitty

By the end of the first month of work, I had sorted my knowledge of Smitty into mental piles for easy access and retrieval. I knew her real first name, which was handy when I needed to decide whether the person on the other end of the phone was a personal friend or a business contact. I knew, in detail, why she and her husband had split up, and also how many people she had slept with in the interim. I knew every member of her family by name, knew how many abortions each of her friends had had, and knew that she insisted on singing along to the radio with a scat-influenced jazz lilt that never changed, no matter what the tune. I also knew some things that she didn't actually tell me—that she was living well beyond her means, for one, and that she was wildly concerned with appearances.

What she knew about me I'm less sure of. Probably that I was a good listener; that we liked a lot of the same music; that I was unhappy with my boyfriend. When I think back to the disjointed first months of our work-focused friendship, I know there were times when she stopped trying to shock me or impress me, times when Smitty was thoughtful and empathetic, times when we barreled through discussions about our families, about books, about the masterful oeuvres of Ella Fitzgerald and Sarah Vaughn. But I don't remember telling her much at all. It was much easier to just listen.

In thinking about my history of dangerous friends, I can only assume that I was drawn to them not only for what they offered—the excitement and spontaneity of, for instance, not knowing whether an evening out would end with us eating fries at an all-night diner or making out with a stranger in another state—but for what I brought to the friendship: namely, the ability to become an instant sidekick to someone more outgoing, more positive, more boy-crazy, and more needy than me. Playing the Rhoda to their Mary, the Shirley to their Laverne is something I've always been good at. A combination of innate shyness, lukewarm self-esteem, and a steady supply of both sarcasm and decent marijuana makes me a pretty good passive friend. I make few demands on the people I hang out with, am up for anything if it's not too convoluted or expensive, and can usually be counted on to be home late at night, watching television, should anyone have a problem to discuss.

After a few months on the job, I had what amounted to a bachelor's degree in Smittyology and a friendship with someone who seemed to value me not only for my skills in the realm of sidekick, but for my skills, period. I quickly moved on to the graduate program, which involved meeting the people on the other end of the phone line.

Smitty's crowd consisted of best friends and former best friends demoted to just friends, ex-boyfriends, business associates, siblings, parents, guys she'd met while perusing African drums on Haight Street, fancy girls she'd gone to school with and now claimed to hate, blind dates, and people from the dog park. Among them was an inner circle of longtime friends, and it was for that inner circle that she seemed to be grooming me.

In gestures of grandiose generosity, she built me up to each and every one of them. "This is Andi," she would say. "She owns her own magazine." As she floated away, I would explain that a friend and I had started a magazine, but it was, in fact, a tiny, struggling enterprise. Or, she would introduce me to someone else by bragging, "Andi's the music editor of the *San Francisco Chronicle*," when the reality was that I wrote a music column for a free weekly. If she was trying to embarrass me, it worked; if she was trying to flatter me, it worked as well—she wasn't concerned with the scale of what I was doing, just the fact that I was doing it. In a time when everyone I knew seemed to be judging everyone else on the size of their success, I couldn't help but appreciate her attempts, careless as they were, at making me seem special.

My first impression of Smitty and her crowd, garnered at one of her many impromptu dinner parties, was that they were like the Algonquin Round Table, but with organic vegetables rather than glasses of gin. They talked about books, film, food, sex. They gossiped voluptuously. They went en masse to fancy restaurants when someone had a birthday, and roasted the birthday girl or boy with dirty laughter and sincere glee. My own evenings tended to consist of morosely splitting a burrito with my boyfriend at the closest taqueria, being careful not to cross the line in the guacamole; by comparison, life at Smitty's place felt warm and lush, mean and comforting. It was as though I'd had my nose pressed to the glass of a more satisfying social life up until now, and I'd finally made my way in.

At the center of it was Smitty. She was brash and rowdy, prone to suddenly streaking buck naked through one of her own parties, pinching other people's butts on her speedy trajectory. She was equally inappropriate in public (where she was as likely as not to belch in your ear or loudly announce her own farts) and in private (where she often indulged the politically questionable habit of making prank phone calls in exaggerated Chinese or Indian accents). She was vulgar, obnoxious, self-centered, and weirdly magnetic.

And, of course, dangerous. Though she wasn't the first dangerous friend I'd had, she was the first who seemed dangerous in a permanent, adult kind of way. Her past was cluttered with enemies; nearly everywhere we went, there was someone she would point out as being "my ex–best friend" or "this guy I used to be so close with." At every party, there was someone who would invariably be blacklisted by the next one. She talked endlessly to me about her other friends, dishing the dirt on their psychological quirks, their neediness, their bad choices in sex partners or clothing. When I met these friends, I often felt that what I knew about them was glowing brightly on my face, and I would have to feign interest in another glass of wine or the bathroom to get away. In retrospect, there was no way to know whether it was all true or whether the things she told me were simply fraught with the very same dramatic embellishment she used to talk me up.

Late one night, Smitty and I sat in her car in front of my apartment building, mid-powwow. She was going through another breakup—a re-breakup, in fact, with the man who had broken up her marriage—and was worried that she was pregnant by him. "I wanted to talk to you about it earlier tonight," she explained, then sighed. "But I didn't want Marie to hear. Marie's not a safe friend for me. I don't feel like I want her knowing my business; it makes me too vulnerable."

I nodded knowingly; only days before, I'd said virtually the same thing to another friend about Smitty. A few years had gone by since our friendship began, and I'd begun regretting the things I'd told Smitty. In good friendships, you tell someone something and feel that what you've said—be it a secret or simply an opinion—deepens their understanding of you. In the case of the dangerous friend, telling her something is equivalent to handing her a loaded gun that will, eventually, be turned straight back at you.

With Smitty, I often ended up telling her the very things I meant not to, simply because there were times when the dangerous part of her seemed to bleed out, leaving a sympathetic, accessible confidant behind. I'd often look at the public version of my friend—the spectacle-creating, never-serious, drag-out-your-worst-feature-in-public Smitty—and realize that I'd sooner entrust the heroin addict peeing on my front steps with my inner Sturm und Drang. But then the one-on-one Smitty would show up, and suddenly I'd find myself detailing my own past pregnancy scares while she reassured me that she'd always be there for me, regardless of what decisions I made. At times like these, I felt buoyed in a way I rarely did with other friends, and then I'd feel bad that I was ever reluctant to trust her.

It was clear, though, that after more than four years, our relationship was foundering. I no longer worked for her, but with her—we'd both been hired by a larger company, and after a few years there she was leaving. To say I was relieved was putting it mildly. She was difficult to work with one-on-one, between the bossiness and the telephone exhibitionism, but in the context of a larger team she'd become almost unbearable. I would occasionally spend my lunch hours consoling her assistant, who'd sob into a tiny salad while telling me what I already knew: that Smitty would tell her to do something and later deny she'd done so; that she gave terrible directions and got mad when her employees couldn't read her mind; that she took credit for other people's work; and that she acted like you were crazy when she was confronted with her behavior.

In a way, it was a relief to learn that not everyone loved her. It came to me as a slow but steady realization—a rolled eye around the worktable, an exchange of glances at a meeting, the use of words like "irritating" and "obnoxious" by the less circumspect of her detractors. It's embarrassing to me now how much of a revelation this was. The self-perpetuating myth within her crowd held that it was a joy simply to be in her presence, but now I was noticing people I liked and respected leaving the room soon after she walked in.

Perhaps it had been that way all the time, but I'd been oblivious to it due to my own feelings of admiration. Now they'd worn off. As with many of my past dangerous friends, my role as the student, the sidekick, and the straight woman had been fun—indeed, educational—but I'd started growing out of it. I began to think I'd been too quick to trust that I'd be a long-term fixture in the life of someone whose personal landscape was littered with ex-friends, enemies, and discarded players in her various dramas.

But it wasn't just that Smitty was a friend to whom, against my clearer judgment, I gave way too much access. If that were all, I wouldn't have worried so much. More important was that I'd begun chafing at her attitude of ownership of me. In a work sense, Smitty felt like she'd made me. And I couldn't deny that her presence in my career had been big, even huge, certainly instrumental, and very positive. But she also took credit for more than her share of what had happened to me—for parts of my personality that had been there all along. She felt like I owed her, and it was starting to come out in the weirdest ways.

On the day of her farewell party, I sat and talked to her about how different work would be without her. "You know," she said suddenly, sharply, "you just like to be bitter and complain." It must have been apropos of something—a reminiscence? a complaint?—and the conversation seemed to flow on smoothly enough once the words had left her mouth, but for the rest of the day they washed back over me in harsh waves. For her the moment was gone, and later, at the farewell party, I watched her air-kissing, circulating, sparkling like a big fake jewel, with no idea of what she'd said or how it had made me feel.

In "How to Dump a Friend," Rosenfeld advises that "the easiest way to dump a friend is not to dump him/her at all, but rather to find a way to live together." For a year or two, I agreed with her. There was the wimp factor, for one thing, but there was also a nagging hope that my friendship with Smitty wasn't, in fact, fraying apart in quite as dramatic a manner as I imagined. Maybe there was a better excuse: We were busy. She was pregnant. I'd gotten a dog, was working increasing hours at both my day job and my magazine, had a new boyfriend with whom I'd begun living.

But every time we spoke or saw one another, it was impossible to deny that, busy or not, things were going badly. I didn't work for her anymore, but she still bossed me around, chastising me about everything from my choice of dog to my boyfriend's job to my yoga regimen. ("It's not really exercise, you know.") For my part, I was still a good listener, but I was delivering my nods and soothing replies less like a caring friend than like one of those plush animals that come programmed with a limited number of phrases: "You just have to give it time." "I wouldn't worry about that—guys are weird." "She's just feeling jealous of you right now; she'll come around."

As the relationship dwindled, I wondered how she really felt. I always assumed she wouldn't miss me when we stopped being friends; it rarely occurred to me that she valued our friendship as anything other than a minor diversion, a mirror reflecting her popularity. I was tired of feeling so fundamentally out of place, tired of feeling like I was a rogue child whose whims she indulged when she was in the mood, but also saw fit to pass constant vocal judgment on. I wanted the madcap Smitty from the early days, or the quiet Smitty who smiled as we sang along together to Ella Fitzgerald on the stereo, our voices trying to emulate the longing that came through the flimsy speakers.

The turning point came the weekend that my boyfriend and I got engaged. I hesitate to make an equation between the two events: It automatically sounds like the worst of all female clichés—the friends who fall out because one gets engaged and the other gets irrevocably jealous. Smitty was pregnant and unmarried to the father of her child, and unprepared for my announcement to come before hers. She grabbed my left hand, inspected the small diamond that perched there, and demanded, "It's fake, right? He got it from one of those machines in the supermarket." I didn't see her for weeks afterward, but the next time I did, she was planning her wedding.

The breakup of a friendship is far less cut-and-dried than most breakups of the romantic variety. The most common breakup isn't a breakup at all, but a long, drawn-out, passive-aggressive matter of unreturned phone calls and e-mails, plans broken at the last minute or made with no intention of following through, and gradual, glacial drifting. Few women will say of a friendship that "it's not the right time for us," or "the thrill is gone," even when these things are completely accurate.

Romantic lives are filled with instances where "he just wasn't right for me," or "the chemistry wasn't there," or "he treated me like shit." Female friendships, on the other hand, are rife with the same situations, but we're expected to treat them differently. My mother and one of her oldest friends, for example, have for decades conducted the kind of on-again, off-again relationship—filled with name calling, telephone hang-ups, and petty gossip—that I assumed died out after junior high. We'll keep up with friends we know aren't good for us, because . . . why, again? Is it the idea that women need women, even when those women treat them as badly as the emotionally abusive boyfriend they'd dump like a moldy doughnut after two bad dates? Is it that we're supposed to value the differences in one another, respect them more, refuse to enforce the deal breakers that regularly sink romances?

I don't know. But in any case, there I was. I'd ended burgeoning relationships with men because they chewed tobacco or owned the *Titanic* soundtrack, but I couldn't end a friendship with someone who had come to belittle nearly everything I did. The thought of breaking up with Smitty seemed like an admission that while I thought I was—or, at least, had once been—a really good friend, I had somehow failed to give enough of myself to keep the friendship going.

Of course I couldn't give enough of myself—I didn't trust her at all and, I kept reminding myself, had been wary about being her friend from the start. Yet the more I agonized about what to do, the more this one ill-starred relationship started seeming like a symptom of my entire friendship life. Maybe being a sidekick wasn't good for either party. Perhaps I chose to melt into the background too much, and perhaps that was why I felt like my friends didn't necessarily know or care that I needed their love and support. Maybe it wasn't anyone's fault but mine.

I folded my clipping of "How to Dump a Friend" and kept it for months in the notebook that held my to-do lists and snippets of writing. I had it when Smitty was admitted a few weeks early to the hospital due to pre-childbirth complications—an event I heard about from everyone but Smitty herself. I had it when I went shopping for a soft purple monkey for her beautiful new daughter. I had it when she airily informed me that she was going to skip my bachelorette dinner.

And I had it when I saw her for what would turn out to be the last time, at my wedding. She came up behind me after family and friends had given their toasts, wrapped her arms around my neck, and whispered something in my ear. It might have been "I'm so happy for you." It might have been "I can't believe you didn't ask me to give a toast." It doesn't matter. What I remember is a fleeting combination of grief and guilt that was there and then gone.

The letter I sent was, in the end, very polite. It was also less of a letter than it was an e-mail—in my last act of Rhoda-esque sidekick considerateness, I made it as easy as possible for Smitty to forward my breakup note to all of her present friends and future ex-friends. We were in different places in our lives, I said, and it was clear that there was no longer much propping up the relationship. I would always have fond memories of her, I noted. It just wasn't the right time for us. I hit Send and went on with my life, stopping only occasionally to wonder if I'd done the right thing. It was only a year later—when I ran into two of Smitty's best friends in a coffee shop and they smirked knowingly at me for what seemed like five hours—that I wished I'd revised the letter, and maybe added a few expletives.

Dinosaur Friends

Alison Krupnick

My three-year-old daughter Melanie was learning about friend-ship—how to make friends, how to keep them, what you can and cannot do with them. There are books about this for preschoolers, I'd discovered. There are books about almost everything for preschoolers. Every afternoon, we'd snuggle up together on our red-and-blue Snoopy beanbag chair and read a book called *How to Be a Friend*. It featured a cast of green dinosaurs.

"What are those girlies doing?" Melanie asked, pointing to a smiling forest-green dinosaur with cornrows holding hands with a gap-toothed, grinning chartreuse dinosaur with a pageboy.

"They're having fun playing together," I said.

"And what about that girl over there? What is she doing?" she asked about a scowling dinosaur.

"She's saying an unkind thing to that boy [olive-green dinosaur in tears] and making him feel sad," I responded.

"And is that okay?" she asked, anticipating my response.

"No," I said, in my best wise and all-knowing parental voice. "It's not okay." We looked at each other and nodded.

At age 40, I was learning about friendship, too—how to make friends, how to keep them, what you can and cannot do with them. When I was younger, friends were mostly recreational. We went to movies and parties and dinners together and occasionally consoled one another about failed love affairs during marathon phone sessions. But now that I was married and at home raising children, friends were my lifeline, my connection to the outside world. I hadn't found any books with dinosaurs to guide me through the process of making this kind of friend.

I'd noticed since becoming a mother that my friendships with other women carried an emotional charge I hadn't experienced since junior high school. Maybe this had to do with hormones left over from pregnancy and lactation. I'd find myself telling near strangers on a playground intimate details of my household affairs at the drop of a hat. You can imagine the scene: Late morning, in a neighborhood park, a mother pushing her toddler in a swing makes eye contact with the mother standing next to her, also pushing a swinging toddler. Shyly, tentatively, they make contact.

"How old is your daughter?"

"Fifteen months. Yours?"

"Seventeen months."

"When did she start walking?"

"About a month ago."

The words come faster. "Now I can't get her to sit in her stroller. Sometimes we need to get somewhere in a hurry and I don't have time to let her walk. But she struggles when I try to put her in the stroller and I have to force her to sit down!"

"Oh, my daughter does that too! It's such a relief to hear that someone else is having the same problem!"

The mothers look at each other, eyes shining, and they're off. Before you know it, they will have exchanged anecdotes about sleep problems, feeding problems, and frustrations with their husbands, and maybe will have even talked about postpartum incontinence, leaking breasts, and changes in sexual arousal. Maybe an intimate friendship will be born from this one morning of shared confidences. Maybe the women will never run into each other again. But no matter how things turn out, you can bet that both women will leave the park feeling better.

The early weeks and months of motherhood can be a lonely time, especially for women who've been working and don't have any close friends who have children. During prenatal yoga and birthing classes, I'd been encouraged to share my feelings, both physical and emotional, with total strangers. Six months or so of sharing on a weekly basis and I was hooked, so I was relieved to learn that post-birth, I would be able to join a community-sponsored moms' support group. I cringe now when I remember the time, not many months into our sessions, when we polled one another to find out who had regained full sensation in her breasts, and the time one woman confessed that she and her husband were having marital problems and were thinking of separating. But during that vulnerable, isolated period of new motherhood, those women were all I had. Those meetings were everything.

One day, one of them called me up. "My kid is driving me crazy and I'm going out of my fucking mind," she said.

"Mine is too!" I said, giddy to hear my frustration so eloquently articulated by someone else, and pleased that I was not the only one trapped at home feeling decidedly unmaternal.

So we went out to lunch. That rendezvous led to another, then another. Another woman from our group began joining us, and soon I had new friends. Several times a week, babes strapped to our bodies, we tooled all over town, exchanging intimacies all the while.

Predictably, as motherhood took hold and these new relationships became more important, older friendships began slipping away. The friend with the jam-packed social life stopped calling with last-minute invitations to fabulous cultural events because I was breastfeeding and couldn't be spontaneous. Unmarried, childless friends from my single days reduced their correspondence with me to an annual Christmas card. My college roommate stopped writing to me altogether. A single male friend with whom I had been very close for several years cut me off without a word. Our last conversation had taken place just after the funeral of his father and my release from the hospital following a pregnancy complication. I sent him a birth announcement to let him know that everything had turned out all right for me. I don't know how things turned out for him; I never heard from him again.

These losses magnified other losses I was feeling—the loss of the spontaneous, independent me who traveled, had a successful international career, and wore decent clothes. If my old friendships ceased to exist, did that mean the old me had also ceased to exist? I thought I had simply added the layers of wife and mother to my core being. Maybe my old friends couldn't find me underneath those layers.

Melanie started preschool. For two-and-a-half years we'd done everything together—moms' group, music classes, gym classes—and we shared a group of mothers and kids as our friends. Now, for the first time, she was in a social situation without me—her first real opportunity to pick her own friends. She spurned her old companions. This worried me. Her teacher told me not to worry. "They don't like mixing friends," she said reassuringly. "At this age, they don't even like mixing different food items on their plates." Melanie talked about the kids in her school with interest, but when I asked who her friends were, she'd say, "Not anyone." Sometimes she'd add, "Nobody likes me!" This worried me even more.

Meanwhile, Annie, a woman I had thought of as a close friend, seemed distant. I didn't understand why. Over the summer we'd played tennis together twice a week and had taken our kids to the same swim class every day for several weeks. We'd supported each other through difficult medical issues, and commiserated about our weight and lack of time for ourselves. But by October, Annie and I hadn't spoken for nearly two months, and although our kids were in the same weekly music class, we hadn't managed to get together afterward. This silence—this lack of intimacy—was eating away at me. I wanted to know what was wrong.

After many sleepless nights I called her up and confronted her. Annie was defensive. She denied that anything had changed. "If you were expecting me to call you twice a week to check in, then maybe we're not a good fit," she said.

"No," I said, "I wasn't expecting that." I confessed that I missed talking to her. I missed sharing the details of our lives. Eventually Annie admitted that she appreciated me as a "mama friend," someone to pass the time with as our kids played with musical instruments or learned to tumble. But she didn't want any more from me than that. I was devastated, wondering how I could have been so wrong in my assessment of the relationship. I felt vulnerable and stupid for having shared so much.

Then, Melanie began coming home from school each day spinning dramatic tales involving a girl named Olivia and their conflicts over a stuffed cat that Melanie had named Splendora. I suggested we use drawings as a way to work through their difficulties.

"Should we draw me playing with Splendora?" Melanie asked. I dutifully obliged.

"Now should we draw Olivia playing with Splendora?" Once again, I complied.

"And now should we draw me taking Splendora away from Olivia?" she said, her voice rising excitedly. I gulped, but did as I was told.

"And should we draw Olivia crying?"

I saw the process through to its conclusion. Over the next several weeks, we drew what seemed like hundreds of renditions of this scene. I refined the process along the way, as my parenting books suggested.

"Should we draw you asking Olivia politely for a turn with Splendora?" Then, "Let's draw both of you smiling and playing together with Splendora."

One Sunday, at our neighborhood coffee shop, we ran into Olivia's parents. I told them their daughter had become a central figure in our household. I didn't go into details. "Olivia has been talking about Melanie, too," they said politely. I smiled to myself, wondering what they were not telling me.

I should have been pleased that Melanie chose this period to become enthralled with the dinosaur friends book. But I was still smarting from my recent rejection by Annie. I felt insecure as I navigated my way through a sea of preschool moms, trying to make new friends. And I missed my original mom friends, whom I rarely saw now that our children were attending different preschools. Night after night, as we read the dinosaur book, I was forced to relearn the rules of friendship: how to overcome your shyness and approach new people, how to make up if you've had a fight, how to find someone else to play with when interests diverge.

At home there was more and more talk of Olivia. Melanie told me that at school, Olivia took Splendora away from her, that she wouldn't let Melanie sit next to her at circle time. But one day, while I was talking on the phone, Melanie got excited. "Who was that, Mommy?" she asked eagerly. "Was that Olivia?"

Soon after, at a school party, we watched as Olivia, a bright-eyed little girl with long dark hair, went bouncing down the hallway. "She's running away from the school!" Melanie exclaimed gleefully, clearly in awe. I could see it by the look on her face. Catfights notwithstanding, Melanie wanted to be Olivia's friend. Maybe I could help her take the first step. I knelt down so that we were at eye level. "Should we invite Olivia over to our house to play?" Melanie looked at me with a half-smile. "Yes," she whispered.

I was circling around some new potential friends myself—people with whom I had things in common other than being a parent, women who wouldn't think of me as just a "mama friend." At a preschool potluck dinner, I talked to Carol and Daniel, the parents of one of Melanie's classmates. I could feel a hint of similar experiences, a complementary outlook on life. So I arranged the Seattle version of an adult play date: We met for coffee. We had not been together for more than five minutes before Carol and I began talking about our relationships with our mothers, while our husbands talked about kiteboarding and our kids played with dominoes. I also began getting together with Alison, a single woman from my writing class. We compared notes about our writing, our travel adventures, and our experiences with long-distance love affairs. I could see the potential these new friends had to enrich my life. Still unsure of the rules of friendship, however, I was careful not to reveal too much.

Olivia came over to play. She and Melanie were polite and careful with each other at first, each waiting to see what the other would do. First one girl and then the other donned a princess dress, a tiara, sparkly shoes. First one girl and then the other reached for a stuffed cat. As one of them declared a preference for something, the other would exclaim, "I like ballerinas, too!" Their eyes sparkled as they discovered more and more common interests—princesses, cats, the color pink. They realized they were kindred spirits.

But then they clashed. I found Melanie in tears in her bedroom, Olivia smiling triumphantly. The stuffed cat they'd had trouble sharing sat between them.

Although it doesn't say so in the dinosaur book, vulnerability is at the heart of friendship. Maybe that's why some friendships can't be sustained over a lifetime. We want to forget our earlier, more vulnerable selves and anyone that reminds us of them. We don't want to compare ourselves to those who have achieved different milestones in life. We don't want to confront our insecurities. With each new friend, you can reinvent yourself—or at least present your best self. Maybe that's why sharing is safer with strangers.

Two years have passed. Some of my friends from before I had Melanie have resurfaced. Some of my newer friends have slipped away. It's usually nothing personal—we're all busy, we're finding a little more time to pursue our own interests, and in some cases, we just don't need each other as much anymore. I've established a few new recreational friendships just for me, ones that have nothing to do with kids. But it's still hard to find time to maintain them.

Melanie, now five, is the veteran of many play dates and has formed some strong friendships. My heart swells with pride when I see her march confidently onto a playground full of strangers and create an instant bond with another child, who she will later assure me is her new best friend. My heart aches for her when she shrinks, shy and trembling, too nervous to join a familiar circle of singing children. We still spend much of our time with Melanie's friends and their mothers. I usually enjoy myself, pleased to have fallen in with a group of women struggling with the same kinds of compromises as I do. But occasionally I grit my teeth and hope that Melanie's infatuation with a particular kid will fade because I have nothing in common with that child's mother.

Recently, Melanie's three-year-old sister, Maya, has been asking me to read her the dinosaur friends book. As we snuggle up and I introduce Maya to the joys and frustrations of friendship, I realize how much she has to learn, and how far Melanie has come.

Soon Melanie will go to kindergarten and we will have to start all over, making new friends at a new school, perhaps losing our connection to the preschool families we've come to like so much. They say that when you're watching your children learn how to make friends, you relive all of your old anxieties about friendship. As it turns out, you get to experience plenty of new ones, too.

Questions for Caren

Juliet Eastland

I entered Boston's Waverly School for Girls in the fifth grade, and by the time I hit the seventh, my identity seemed set: I was the dork, the dark-haired, bespectacled smart kid who ate lunch with an open book in her lap, the gangly girl who was chosen last in gym; and when I grew up I would be an adult dork, just like my dark-haired, bespectacled parents. I understood that my place was on the edges of Waverly's social scene. I was accustomed to the benign neglect of my classmates—blond, blue-eyed girls from the suburbs who fluttered through the hallways like exotic birds—lovely in their field hockey skirts and velvet dancing-school dresses, and drenched in sunny, golf-course colors: corals, lime greens, and madras plaids exploding in tropical hues. While girls chattered about the boys from our brother school, I reveled in my classes: French, where the vowels lilted and undulated off my tongue; social studies, where I would run my hand along my wooden desktop carved with generations of initials and pretend I could feel the heat and smoothness of the pyramids. My books and my imagination kept me company, and I wasn't lonely, or so I thought. Until I met Caren.

Caren entered my class three weeks into the seventh grade, having come up from Georgia after her mother got a new job in Boston. More startling than her abrupt entrance, Caren was black—not inky black, but a light, creamy brown. She wore her hair pulled into a ponytail. Freckles like brown sugar dusted her nose and cheeks, and she wore a gold cross on a thin chain around her neck. I thought she was beautiful. On her first day, our homeroom teacher had to lug in an extra desk and chair from another classroom. Caren's last name began with "K," so her desk had to be squeezed into the third row with those of the other middle-of-the-alphabet students. The girls in her row got up, grumbling, and reluctantly pulled their desks and chairs aside to make space for the new girl. The black girl. Nobody dared look at her directly, but I noticed a lot of sideways glances as girls slid back into their seats. At the end of my row, one of them scribbled something on a note and passed it to her friend, who laughed unkindly. Ahead of me, Caren sat with perfect posture, unmoving, her dark head standing out from the rows of blond ones like a dusky tulip.

Caren's first day was a Monday, always a chaotic day in homeroom. Girls were giddy with the details of their weekend—cigarettes, spin-the-bottle, second base. As usual, I was eavesdropping. One even unbuttoned the placket of her polo shirt to display the hickey on her neck, a fierce-looking red mark that left me even more afraid of boys than I already was. I saw Caren's head swivel a few rows ahead: She was listening, too. The teacher quieted the room and announced an upcoming bake sale for the field hockey team, and next week's field trip to Paul Revere's house. As the bell rang for first period, girls surged to the door, and I found myself wedged against Caren. "I like your sweater," she said shyly. "Purple is my favorite color." We were swept into the hallway. I thanked her and explained that, according to our history textbook, purple was the color that emperors of ancient Rome wore. She smiled at me, and my heart jumped. Suddenly, it felt like a long time since I had made anyone laugh.

"What's your next class?" I asked, willing her not to melt into the crowd. It turned out we were headed to the same math class, so I walked with her down the hall.

"I love math," she confided, which impressed me, as math was not my strong suit.

Caren and I were in several of the same classes, so I became her unofficial guide as she navigated Waverly's halls, narrow passageways that looked as if they hadn't been renovated since the school's founding in 1886. It was the first time a classmate had relied on me for anything, and I felt a rush of joy at being needed. Caren and I had another thing in common: We were two of the few students who lived nearby and weren't bused in from the suburbs.

We began meeting outside school after our last class and walking the half-mile home together. Caren's house had better junk food than mine, so we would raid her kitchen for peanut butter and marshmallow fluff on Wonder Bread, Oreos from the package, and a bowl of whatever ice cream happened to be in the freezer. Caren would put on one of her mother's records—Marvin Gaye, the Staple Singers, Ashford & Simpson. When Caren first put on James Brown's "I Feel Good," with its ferocious beat, I felt as if I would explode with excitement. (At my house, we listened to American musicals and opera.) With the music pulsing in the background, we would settle in at the kitchen table and hunker down over our homework. Caren would help me with my math equations, her head bent next to mine, pencil hovering over the worksheet. I marveled at how she looked at a geometric shape and seemed to understand how the lines and angles fit together. Sometimes I would get so frustrated I would slam the pencil down, breaking the point, and Caren would lay her hand on mine.

"You'll get it," she reassured me. "Just go slow, and write it all out."

She, on the other hand, never got the hang of French, so I would help her with that homework. Sometimes I would balance a pencil on my upper lip like a *Fronsch moostache* and imitate her Southern accent, but in French, and we'd laugh so hard we would have to lay our heads down on the kitchen table. I never saw Caren laugh like this with anyone else; our classmates left her alone at school, and I'd seen girls in the lunchroom grow silent as we approached. Sometimes I would hear whispering begin as we passed, and it felt as though their eyes were burning my back. I knew it was because I was with Caren, the black girl. My face would flush, but Caren would move forward, her posture perfect, conceding nothing. We never spoke about the whispering, and eventually I convinced myself that she never noticed.

Caren and I talked about everything. She told me about how, before her parents got divorced, her father would leave home for weeks at a time, eventually moving into an apartment a few miles away. I was fascinated. My dad came home late from work a lot, but I knew it wasn't the same thing. Neither of us had gotten our periods, and we debated whether a casual observer would be able to tell when we did. I thought not, but Caren was convinced that we would look different. She could never explain how. "I don't know, more . . . grown-up." Her brow furrowed. We had both devoured *Are You There God? It's Me, Margaret,* and were prepared to shed delighted tears at the first sight of menstrual blood. Caren told me she had French-kissed a boy in Georgia, and I squealed as she described how his tongue had flopped like an eel in her mouth and how she'd wanted to throw up on his sneakers.

That Christmas vacation, Caren invited me to go with her to spend a weekend at her father's house in New York. I lobbied my parents at dinner, and when Caren's mother called our house to get permission, my parents didn't have any objections. Caren's mother took us to Back Bay Station and waved us off as we boarded the train. "Have a good time, sweetheart. Make sure you get some sleep," she murmured, hugging Caren and burying her face in her hair. "Be good, okay?" She turned to me, and her face closed into a polite smile. "Have fun," she said lightly. She didn't touch me. Caren's mother always made me uncomfortable; it was as if there were wheels turning in her head, processes happening that I couldn't understand. I was glad when the train rumbled forward and all of it—Caren's mother, the station platform, Boston—receded out of view.

Caren and I stayed for two nights with her father on Roosevelt Island, a little enclave connected to Manhattan by a cable car. I had never been in a condominium, and I thought this one looked like a heaven for men—all beiges and grays, masculine and glamorous, with a sparkling view of the Manhattan skyline. Caren's father, a handsome bachelor, treated us as though we were adult houseguests who didn't need any guidance from him. "Here's $100 for the weekend," he announced when we arrived, handing Caren a crisp bill. "The city is your oyster. Enjoy!" We bought Sun-In and spritzed our orange hair, our streaked dark heads like a sunset painted on black velvet. We took the cable car into Manhattan by ourselves and wandered along Canal Street through the frosty air, arm in arm, in love with the world and with each other. We stopped at a sidewalk vendor's display and bought gaudy rhinestone clip-on earrings and fastened them onto each other's ears, laughing. With her earlobes sparkling, Caren seemed to glitter like the city itself.

We returned to Boston, where snow dusted the ground. School started, and Caren and I resumed our routine of homework, music, and snacks. A few weeks into the term, I tapped the girl sitting in front of me in homeroom and passed her a note for Caren: *Wanna go to the mall after school Friday?* The mall was a few subway stops away, and it was home to Spencer's, purveyor of lava lamps, light-up key chains, and tiny clip-on koala bears—to us, the greatest store in the world. The note made its way back to me a few minutes later.

Can't . . . I'm busy, she wrote, adding a sad face. I stared at the piece of paper for a moment. It was unusual for either of us to be busy on a Friday afternoon.

I wrote back: *So? Details PLEEEZE!* The note journeyed up the row. I studied Caren's back, as if it would provide a clue to her plans. The note returned.

41

It's this dumb dance thing my mom is making me go to. ACK!
This was Bill the Cat's choice exclamation from our favorite comic,
Bloom County.

My stomach jumped. What dance? I would have heard about a
school dance—girls would have been buzzing about it for weeks. Besides, since when did either of us go to dances? I crumpled up the
note and shoved it in my pocket.

Caren and I met up outside homeroom and linked arms as we
walked to math class. As we neared the classroom, I took a deep
breath. "So what's this dance you're going to?" We paused outside
the door.

"It's this thing my mom signed me up for." Caren shifted her
books in her arms. "It's a social thing. It sounds really dumb. It's for
black kids." Caren spoke without meeting my gaze. She was looking
just to the side of me, and I felt a rush of invisibility. The word "black"
hung in the air, taking longer to dissipate than the rest of the sentence. It was the first time either of us had acknowledged out loud the
racial difference between us. I realized that we hadn't talked about
everything, not quite. Black and white hadn't been relevant to our
friendship—or so I'd thought. All of a sudden, I wasn't so sure. Our
classmates swirled around us, jostling and chattering, but for a moment I heard only silence. I stared at the gold cross on its chain,
nestled in the valley of Caren's throat, and leaned against the door-
jamb for balance.

"Oh!" I finally expelled a breath. "Jeez, I guess I can't be your date,
huh?" We laughed. "Okay, so Saturday, then," I said. "A movie. *The
Thin Man* is coming to the Arledge."

"Um, I can't. It's the whole weekend. It's this retreat thing—it's the
first weekend of this whole program, so they're taking our parents
and us out to some town in the boonies. We'll probably do things like
that dumb ropes game. The dance is on Saturday."

"Ladies!" It was our teacher, calling us in for class. We took the
last two remaining seats across the room from each other. I tried to con-

centrate on the equations on the blackboard, but my eyes kept darting until they settled, like a compass needle, on Caren. She nibbled on her pencil eraser as she puzzled out the problems. I examined the top of her head. The orange streaks had started to grow out, and her dark hair was coming in at the roots. I considered the fact that she had made plans without me. Would she meet a boyfriend? A new best friend? My insides churned, and I shifted in my seat. Mrs. Taft caught my eye and nodded toward the board. I bent down over my paper. Maybe things weren't as bad as I thought. It was just some weekend event. So why did I feel my world had just gotten drastically smaller?

We spent that weekend apart, Caren at her black-kids retreat and I at the movie theater, curled morosely in a red velvet chair while Nick and Nora traded wisecracks on the screen. The glittering skyline outside their apartment window reminded me of Caren's father's condominium. Roosevelt Island seemed a million miles away.

That Monday in homeroom, I waited for Caren to share her weekend with me. Nothing. Near the end of the period, I scribbled a note—*Carinna! You missed* The Thin Man *this weekend! How was the ropes course?* I chose the language carefully. The tone had to be just right—no big deal.

The note came back to me: *Jujubee! I'm so sad I missed the movie! Sno-Caps . . . popcorn mmm. . . .* She didn't answer my question.

Over the next few weeks, Caren and I continued walking home together, but we started parting ways at her street corner, and I would walk down my street slowly, in case she called me back. I wondered who was helping her with her French. My math homework was suffering, but when I told her this in a mock-pathetic tone, she gave my arm a squeeze but did not offer to help. I joined the choir, mostly because it took my mind off Caren, but also because it met after class two days a week, which meant I wouldn't have to face rejection every day. I formed a desultory friendship with the girl next to me, but her perky good spirits grated on me, and I hated the madrigals we were singing. There were days where I didn't see Caren at lunch hour, and I would sit with the girls from choir, thinking about Caren, wondering if she was avoiding me or even skipping lunch entirely. Caren's program took up every weekend, and I stopped trying to make weekend plans with her. Eventually I stopped asking about her weekends altogether.

A few weeks before the school year ended, Caren caught up with me after math class and told me that she and her mother would be moving away over the summer. Caren would be going to another prep school, a few hours north of Boston. I knew that most of the students at the school were black. I wanted to ask Caren what would happen to all the new friends she had presumably made this year, but I swallowed the question. I wasn't sure I had the right to ask it. We hugged each other, and Caren promised to write and tell me about the boys in her class.

That evening, I stared at my social studies textbook, the words wavering in and out of focus. I finally closed the book and ripped out a blank sheet of paper from my notebook. I wrote QUESTIONS FOR CAREN at the top of the page. I knew that our friendship, our passion, had been real. So why did race matter? More specifically, why did race end up mattering to her, but not to me? Why did it *have* to matter? I turned the word "freedom" over in my mind. Did Caren and I have different degrees of freedom in the world? Freedom from what, or for what? Freedom to choose our friends? To ignore a difference in skin color? My head ached, and I couldn't get any closer to articulating what I meant by these amorphous, uncomfortable questions. I yearned to call my soul mate. I wanted to tell her how much I missed her. I wanted to win her back. I wanted to convey to her how complicated our world now felt to me. I wanted to apologize, to confess it was only now that I realized that her world must have been this complicated all along.

I finally wrote, *Why did you choose?* Then I scribbled out the words and wrote, *Why did you feel like you had to choose?* I drew a sad face next to the question mark. I read the sentence out loud. It sounded meaningless. The sheet of lined paper, the penciled words across the top—none of it seemed to have anything to do with the way our lives had just shifted. I tucked the note inside my binder. I decided I would send it to Caren if she ever wrote me from her new school, but she never did.

Lizzy

by Ariel Schrag

Evidence

Jacqueline Lalley

Quick: Which side does your best friend wear her purse on? It's a test I would have failed at any time during my fifteen-year friendship with Kirsten. But now I know: On this rust-colored suede jacket, it's the right shoulder that's worn through. I don't plan to mend it. It keeps her close by and alive in some way, this spot she passed her bag over every day.

Kirsten disappeared. Her friends and family haven't heard from her in more than five years. We all know what happened to her. We know she's dead, we know who killed her, we know where he lives.

Her clothes, chosen with her glorious and occasionally baroque sense of style, hang around our houses or lie at the bottom of drawers. We touch them—and some, like me, wear them. And we feel guilty.

Kirsten lived in New York. At age twenty-eight, she was five months pregnant, the result of a single sexual encounter with Ranajay—known as Jay. I remember how excited she was about him at first. He was one of her teachers at the college where she was a semester away from a pre-law degree in philosophy. They'd flirted, but he waited until the semester was over to ask her out. He was handsome—no, "adorable," she said. And he had a real career. She thought of him as a serious prospect, not like the many men she'd had passionate—but ultimately casual—relationships with: waiters, rock musicians, security guards.

When Kirsten told Jay she was pregnant, he got a shock—but she got an even bigger one: After they'd had sex, he'd gotten married. Two weeks after they'd slept together, he'd gone away on what he'd said was a business trip. It was actually his honeymoon. The ceremony had been long planned, the match arranged by relatives. He and his bride were part of the same tight-knit ethnic community. His wife was the daughter of a priest. If Kirsten had the baby, he said, it would ruin his life. He would be disgraced and disowned. He begged her to have an abortion.

Kirsten was pro-choice. Growing up in Madison, Wisconsin, "a woman's right to choose" had been a truism for us. In fact, she'd had several abortions. But New York wasn't Madison. The chaotic mélange of her new home gave her permission to interrogate her past assumptions, to explore and evolve—that's why she loved it there. Around the time she got involved with Jay, she'd been reading and thinking critically about women's bodies and the ethical and philosophical implications of abortion. For Kirsten, there was no artifice, no line between her studies and her life. In one of our last conversations, she argued that her own abortions hadn't been motivated by the interests of the child, but by her self-interest. Women had had babies in much harsher conditions, hadn't they? I couldn't tell if she was just playing the devil's advocate or if she believed her own argument. That's the way Kirsten was: Disagreeing with her only made her defend her position more passionately. She was going to be a great lawyer.

She'd told Jay during their one encounter that they'd better be careful—that if she got pregnant, she was having the baby. Later, she came to think of the conception as something of a miracle. She didn't say it was about atonement, but I think in part it was. Kirsten was committed to raising the child with or without Jay.

I've thought a lot about the irony of Kirsten's death: As feminists, we fight hard to defend a woman's right to choose not to become a parent. But apparently, choosing motherhood can be equally dangerous. According to an MSNBC special on Kirsten that aired in July 2001, a woman who is or was recently pregnant is more likely to be the victim of homicide than to die of any other cause. It seems that the right to choose is only a right when we make the "correct" choice—one that's convenient for the man.

Kirsten and I had reached a point in our friendship where we talked on the phone just a few times a year. She lived in New York, I lived in Chicago; I didn't like to admit it, but we'd drifted apart. I'd left Madison for Massachusetts in the early '90s to go to college, and later moved to Chicago to be with my then-boyfriend and get a job. She'd moved to Atlanta and then to New York, working at restaurants and making new friends.

The year before her disappearance, as Kirsten threw herself into her studies in New York, our friendship changed. Suddenly, we were talking on the phone about philosophy, history, even poetry. She called in a panic because a B might throw off her 4.0 GPA. To be honest, I felt a little threatened by her burgeoning interest—and success—in academia. Back in high school and in our early 20s, I had been the intellectual, the stereotypical brunette to redheaded Kirsten and blond Delia. They were social dynamos who had succeeded in an area where I had repeatedly failed—sexual conquest. Whereas I was incapable of all but the most cerebral of flirtations, and compulsively implanted myself in long-term relationships, they got the guys, lots of them, the kind who slept till noon and wore knit hats in July—the kind for whom commitment was more important in a bass player than in a girlfriend.

Before all that, even before Kirsten introduced me to Delia, it was a (paradoxically) shared sense of not-belonging that brought the two of us together in what I've come to think of as a fragile time. And not just for us—it was the era of Reagan, the nuclear arms race, and *The Morning After.* We spent our time together talking about sex (Kirsten had experience, I had questions), drinking Boone's Farm copped off of friends who were legal, but also doing all this kids stuff: calling each other "stupe-dig" (as in, "My mama didn't raise no stupe-dig"), repeating pet phrases ("fuck a goddamned clucky duck"), and developing nicknames of complicated evolution (for a period during high school, everyone had to call her "Arthamese"). She had a collection of 45s that included the Monkees, Tiny Tim, a rhapsodic and obscure ode to Canada, and a Senator Everett McKinley Dirksen sound-alike singing "Wild Thing." But didn't we also listen to Sade, the Police, Cindy Lauper, Elvis Costello, and the Ramones? In my mind, right next to the memories of trick-or-treating together (tell me you didn't try it in high school) are flashes of staying up all night at a party drinking wapatoolie (the alcoholic equivalent of the "grog soup" I'd had at Girl Scout camp) served out of a trash can, then watching the sun rise over Lake Mendota. Summer nights, we'd wander the near-east side of Madison, stealing toilet paper from Supreme Pizza, breaking into the soccer field to play hide-and-seek with some guys, and climbing a ladder to sit and talk on a tennis court atop the water-treatment plant.

In social situations, Kirsten saved me, pulling me out from under the weight of my shyness and sharing her limelight with me. We used our own repartee, rife with in-jokes and sarcasm, to engage guys—who, if they proved dull or scary, could be excluded by the same means. Kirsten's attitude was that no one was her equal until proven otherwise. Having passed that test, as I had somehow managed, I felt like I held a VIP pass. Together, we moved on to things like jobs, veganism, and recreational drugs.

In 1998, we reconnected after a few years of not much contact. Because of all of the changes we'd gone through, we had to learn new ways of relating. It was challenging, but it was good; our friendship had

Evidence

a future. With both of us in school (undergraduate for her, MFA for me), our conversations had evolved beyond the subjects of adolescent obsession (guys and other women). And there was the baby. I was looking forward to my transition to Aunt Jackie, and lobbied for her to move to Madison so I could be more active in dispatching my duties of choosing baby clothes and, down the line, offering advice on which boys (or girls) to date, whether liking girls (or boys) meant you were gay, and which drugs to do only in the woods with people you love.

We talked twice during her pregnancy—first when she told me she was going to have a baby. That's when I got the description of Jay as dreamy, her serious prospect. The next time we spoke, things had gotten weird. After they'd dropped their mutual bombshells—she was pregnant, he was married—he avoided her. He wasn't teaching at the college anymore. As was customary in his community, he lived with his parents, and his wife had moved in. The only way to contact him was by pager, and he usually didn't return calls.

Months went by without Kirsten hearing from Jay, and it was driving her crazy. She didn't need him to be involved in the baby's life, but she didn't want him cut out, either. She wanted them to put down on paper what they both wanted and then get a lawyer to help them make a binding agreement. On Kirsten's list were minimal financial support and as much contact with the child as Jay wanted. Jay never made a list. Once, in a rare phone conversation, he said he was willing to go to a lawyer, and would pick her up that Sunday and take her to see one—in a bad neighborhood, she told me. She said okay, then got scared and backed out. She told her sister, other friends, and me that she didn't want to be in a car alone with him. "What lawyer has Sunday appointments—in that part of town?" she said.

Something else happened. He told her he was in trouble at home—his wife knew about Kirsten and the pregnancy and was threatening to kick him out. He needed to see her; he needed her support. Kirsten's roommates remember him coming over. It was one of the few times they met at her apartment instead of at a café or restaurant. Jay offered to make her a soymilk-and-fruit shake, knowing the shakes were part of her prenatal diet. She got sick after she drank it; on the phone with me, she said she was afraid he was trying to poison her.

Imagine living 800 miles from a friend and hearing all of this. A couple of months ago, he was a dream come true. Now she's afraid to get in the car with him? And she thinks he's poisoning her? A large part of me was sure she was being paranoid—maybe it was the prenatal hormones. Another part of me read the news. To be on the safe side, I pressed her to just avoid him.

But Kirsten, again, was willful. She had her mind set on working something out with Jay before the baby was born, so she kept in contact with him as much as she could. She promised to be careful. But she also told her friend Sally, "If anything happens to me, Jay did it."

I never spoke to Kirsten after she told me about the shake incident. Weeks later, on October 25, 1998, I got a phone message from her brother. All it said was that he wanted to know the last time I'd talked to Kirsten.

Talking with her sister Katie on the phone, I learned that Jay had lured Kirsten to meet with him by claiming his wife had kicked him out, that he was homeless and Dumpster-diving, and wanted her help cleaning an apartment he was going to rent. Against her better judgment, Kirsten got into Jay's car with him and rode off.

The next couple of days were a confused panic. I went to work but kept my door closed. I'd mindlessly abide my routine for up to an hour at a time, then suddenly feel sick with horror and visceral disbelief. I compulsively imagined one possible course of events and then another, writing in my journal:

> Scenarios: Kirsten dead in an abandoned building. Kirsten alive and captive in the New York area, or in Jay's home country, where her baby will be born and taken from her. Kirsten dead and buried. I struggle to force myself to not say

> she is dead. . . . These ideas are so horrible I find myself not
> thinking of Kirsten at the center of them, but of a third per-
> son, a character in a movie. Kirsten, meanwhile, is where she
> has been—safe in the arms of the past, untouchable.

When I told my boss what was happening, and that the police were sitting on the case because they thought, idiotically, that Kirsten had just wandered off, she said media attention was the only thing that would mobilize them. "Pitching" Kirsten's murder to the press felt crass. But I spent the next day at the fax machine with a stack of news releases (in a Wonder Woman costume, no less—our office Halloween party was in progress). That night, Kirsten's face was on every New York TV station. The next day, the police began their investigation, and I got on a plane to New York.

The one-bedroom apartment where Katie lived with her husband and their toddler was crammed full of people and baggage. There were fellow students, coworkers from the Jamaican restaurant where Kirsten waited tables, neighbors, ex-boyfriends, and, of course, family. Kirsten was—had been—the youngest. Her brother and other sister had come from Madison. Katie was in overdrive, answering the phone, haranguing the police, giving media interviews, and trying to keep us from doing anything stupid.

Kirsten's mother was too overwhelmed by shock, grief, and confusion to come. She told me a few months later that she'd often listen to Schoenberg's *Verklaerte Nacht,* which reminded her of Kirsten, and "cry and cry." I bought the CD but still can't bring myself to unwrap it. Every time we talk, she says, "Say hello to your mother for me; she's such a nice person."

For me, the one positive thing that has come of Kirsten's disappearance is the bond I've formed with several women who were close to her— some of whom I met only after she was gone.

Delia, Kirsten, and I were friends growing up in Madison. Delia has pale-blond hair, bright blue eyes, and—for the past 15 years—an inoperable brain tumor. (Between her and Kirsten, I sometimes feel I'm next in line for a personal tragedy.) She's a graphic artist and is my model of generosity and unconditional love. Despite the tumor, she lives a pretty normal life. Everyone falls in love with her.

Sally was a fellow student at the college who saw Jay plenty of times and heard all about him from Kirsten. Like Kirsten, Sally is adventurous, flirtatious, and a redhead. Born to Irish parents, she's a lifelong New Yorker, complete with a tiny, inherited apartment. When I met her, after Kirsten's disappearance, she was in her first semester of an MFA in fiction, and I'd just finished my MFA in poetry. I've nagged her to send me her work, but she's never done it. She's one of the most talented writers I've never read.

Grace, with whom Kirsten had shared an apartment in Atlanta, is yet another redhead, and a bad-boy magnet at that. She works in film and video, and has documented our benefits and protests having to do with Kirsten's disappearance. I only met her briefly while Kirsten was still alive. Even then, she struck me as artistic but firmly grounded—a dependable friend. I wish I could watch a video of her and Kirsten hanging out, so I could see how they related.

Kirsten spent a lot of time with her sister Katie and her family in New York. I don't remember ever meeting Katie when we were kids. She's a teacher and mentor for at-risk teens. For several years, she made finding Kirsten a second full-time job. She's spent a large part of her savings on private investigations and has tried everything from psychics to billboards. I look at her and think, How has she survived? If this happened to my sister, how would I?

The five of us have gotten together several times since 1998, mainly to work on Kirsten's case. At first, together with a large group of Kirsten's family members and friends, we spread the word and pressured the police. We held vigils and rallies and posted notices of a reward for information. Katie got a friend to create a website. We worked with a private investigator. We organized a benefit concert back in Madison, with bands Kirsten used to like. In 1999, we went to her graduation; her college granted her degree in absentia, to her mother. That year, our group of five began its tradition of getting together on the anniversary of her disappearance.

The case remains unsolved: The police are going through the infuriatingly slow process of "building a case," which involves not only gathering information and searching for physical evidence, but doing it in a way that will make for a successful trial. For the first year, I think a lot of us stayed open to the possibility that Kirsten was alive. Now I don't think anyone really harbors that hope. I don't think of seeing her alive or holding her anymore—in fact, that seems morbid, somehow. Instead, I think of the moment when I can see my friend's bones and know she's really gone. I wonder if I will have any tears left, any grief. But I want the chance to find out. The urge to achieve closure, as clichéd as it has become, is very strong.

In the meantime, we five have become close. In New York, we've gone shopping at flea markets, sari shops, and a discount clothing outlet Kirsten used to call Cheap Shit (think nylon, synthetic fur, and a fitting room just for drag queens). We've been to the hair salon and the gym. Grace has come to Chicago to visit, and I talk to Delia every month or so—more often than I used to talk to Kirsten. We all e-mail, especially as the anniversary approaches. Katie, the driving force behind all of the work to find Kirsten and the one who's in touch with the police, is the hub of our friendship.

I feel I can discuss anything with these women. And yet, our intimacy is sometimes flawed and nervous, as if we were making conversation while waiting for Kirsten to come back from the bathroom. I find myself holding back, wanting to keep them in their roles as Kirsten's supporting characters (except for Delia, with whom I developed a separate friendship long ago). Maybe I'm afraid that if I allow them to fill the spot I've been keeping open for Kirsten in the middle of our circle, I'll have to admit that she will never come back.

Even as our friendships have deepened, guilt gets in the way of my being able to totally relax with them—anxiety over being unable to solve this problem over which I have no control. And there's an absence of convention and protocol. What are these friendships if based on the mutual love of a woman who is not alive and not dead? Are we to console or be consoled? Are we allowed to be happy together?

I realized some time ago that I was trying to divest my relationships with these women of fun, as if having fun meant I didn't miss Kirsten or wasn't working hard enough to—well, to bring her back. I've had many irrational thoughts about what I can do or could have done to keep Kirsten in our lives. I wrote in my journal:

> I remember deciding, on the very day Kirsten was last seen,
> that I would send her a birth-preparation book I'd picked up.
> If I had sent it, if I had begun that arc, wouldn't she have to
> appear to complete it?

But as I've allowed them, Kirsten's friends have helped me learn that real friendship precludes the need to prove my value by doing the impossible. I can entrust them with something no one else understands—my memories of Kirsten—and I've begun to understand that that's what I offer them, too.

One anniversary, we gathered in Katie's new apartment (she and her husband had separated, a large factor being the strain of the disappearance) and read Kirsten's old journals. She was a thorough, compulsive journal-keeper, much more consistent than I am. And what did I do, faced with this chronicle of years we'd shared and years we'd been apart? Like any other red-blooded American woman, I scoured them for passages about me—specifically, for some definitive declaration that I, and not our other friends, was her favorite. I chalked this up to human psychology and tried to get the others to admit they were doing the same, but they wouldn't. Or they weren't. (I did find one: When Kirsten was about thirteen, she wrote that of her three closest friends, I was her "best friend." The victory felt decidedly hollow.)

Another year, we did something I dreaded—divvied up her clothes. Thus the suede jacket with the worn right shoulder, the short green silk dress, a few embroidered sleeveless shirts, and lots of other things that the committee deemed me worthy of (many by virtue of my small size) came to me. Her clothes filled many trash bags; we had to give some to charity, even as we imagined Kirsten's wrath. Clothing went way beyond function or even fashion for her. Her clothes spoke for her in profound ways: Without the right outfit, she felt wretched, despicable. And "right" might be a flared, ankle-length burgundy velvet skirt, sewn by her mother; a nerdy plaid dress; or the new, knee-high black leather boots she wore on her last trip out of the apartment.

Delia doesn't wear Kirsten's things; of all of us, I think she's the only one who still holds some remote—perhaps even unconscious—hope that Kirsten will return. I have Delia to thank for the pendant, a silver flower with a green glass globe at the center. She took it—along with a ring for herself and similar jewelry for Grace and Sally—from Kirsten's room the day after the police had started their investigation. We were under strict orders not to touch anything. I was afraid to disobey, so all I could bring myself to do was write down the titles of all of the books on her shelves. (Some of those titles are listed here.) That list, in a way, is a portrait of Kirsten on October 24, 1998—of the childhood friend I was getting to know again, in all of her new aspects, when suddenly, she disappeared.

The Foot Book (Dr. Seuss)
The New Skepticism
I, Rigoberta Menchu
Imagine There's No Heaven
Animal Liberation
Science versus Religion
The Path to Love

The Sexual Politics of Meat
Yoga for Pregnancy
New York, Naturally: A Directory
The Politics of Reality
The Miracle of Mindfulness
Reproduction, Ethics, and the Law
The Inferno (Pinsky)
What to Expect When You're Expecting
Dependency and Development
The Confessions of St. Augustine
Parents Magazine
Born Dead
The Philosophy of Right and Wrong
The Philosophy of Horror
35,000 Baby Names
They Won't Take Me Alive

Prima

Myriam Gurba

I t was the summer before I began ninth grade at St. Bernadette High School. My parents had chosen it because the girls there looked nice—blue plaid skirts, white blouses, and crisp white knee socks. Bern's girls were confined; we weren't allowed to leave campus like the kids at the public school across the street. At noon, those kids would cram into little VW Bugs or old pickup trucks and go eat lunch at the Jack in the Box. They'd have hot fries and bacon cheeseburgers and onion rings. And they'd top it all off with a couple of bong hits in the restaurant's parking lot, then return to school with dreamy blood-shot eyes and a nagging stoner's hunger. They weren't bad kids, though. Bern's girls were. We had dirty secrets you couldn't see, and nobody knew it better than the boys across the street. "Bern's girls'll give you the burns," they would whisper.

That summer, my cousin came to stay with us. Coquette was the daughter of Aunt Vicky, my Dad's baby sister. Vicky wanted to get Co-quette out of L.A. because she blamed it, *la ciudad de los angeles*, for incubating her daughter's latent criminal tendencies. My cousin's Daddy had been an old-school gangster, or so I'd heard. From him, Coquette had inherited a blood-fire that created an uncontrollable desire to destroy everything in her path on her way to destroying herself. Vicky watched Coquette's criminal spirit slowly emerge, midwifed by the smog and housing projects that surrounded the two of them. Vicky didn't want Coquette to get sweet on those dangerous streets, to become her father's daughter.

It was Grape Street, a clique of Mexican homegirls who claimed the color purple as their own, who took Coquette by the hand and showed her what it meant to open herself up to violence. These *locas* were the girls who discovered how easy it was to seduce Coquette with something that they didn't have a name for but existed as a kind of sexy nihilism. This thing that the Grape Street *locas* had was like a plant or a flower that could only live in certain places, places shrouded in smog—wet alleys, dry riverbeds, and underneath freeway overpasses. For Coquette, this thing was part aphrodisiac, part street drug, and it hooked her so that the *gangstas* could claim her as their own.

Those *chicas* took her criminal virginity. She was 14 when they baptized her in their shower of smashing fists and broken bottles, devoured her like a tattooed and hairsprayed school of piranhas eating one of its own. The initiation left her with two black eyes—a little beat-up raccoon girl—and a cracked rib that went clear through her chest and poked out through her skin. But it was enduring, this violence that earned her the title of sister and homegirl, that made her an equal to the girls that she had so desperately looked up to.

My aunt figured that maybe the best way to sever the bond between Grape Street and her daughter was to get Coquette out of there, send her away like a knocked-up teenager who goes upstate to have her baby, get some fresh air, and forget about the boy. But it was too late for that. Coquette was like a walking zombie, a numb little robo-chola who never cracked a genuine smile. Deep inside something ugly controlled her and it wanted to claw its way out. My aunt knew that Coquette could erupt at any time. Tears of rage or something worse could come spilling down her cheeks, and my aunt didn't really want to be there when it finally happened. She didn't want to see Coquette as anything but strong, the tough girl who never cried. And that was that.

The box of letters was the last straw for my aunt. She found it under my cousin's bed, heavy and wrapped tightly with colorful rubber bands. The box was full of a lovingly archived correspondence between Coquette and five prison inmates, ranging in ages from 26 to 42, to whom she'd been writing since she was 13. They were Coquette's pen pals, hard, dirty men who had nothing better to do than sit and wait to be amused by letters arriving from curious young homegirls on the outside.

The Grape Street *locas* had encouraged this correspondence. They told Coquette it comforted the *veteranos* who'd been put away for their crimes and belonged to Grape Street's male counterpart, the 16th Avenue Rollers. In her letters, Coquette would ask the inmates what they'd done to get twenty-five to life, and they'd answer her girlishly scrawled questions with the dismissal, "*M'ija*, a fine little *heine* like you don't need to know 'bout such things." They'd describe the loneliness and isolation of being in lockdown, the daily grind of prison life. They'd tell her how they missed the smell and taste of a woman and wonder how she smelled, how she tasted, describing all the things they'd do to her young body if they could have her for only five minutes. These letters were so wrong, so sad and disgusting—but they obviously meant something to Coquette. I think they fed a girlish hunger inside her, gave her somebody to imagine as daddy.

My aunt sent her to us to save her from a lot of things, but we couldn't save Coquette from herself. Vicki wanted to cut the cord between her daughter and the things that were turning her hard, to anchor her in a place that might send the blood pumping back through her veins and make her alive again. That summer, in our little seaside town of Santa Maria, famous along California's central coast for its prolific chicken farms and broccoli acreages, she slept in my room on a little bed beside mine. My job was to guide her back to teenage normalcy or somewhere like it. I was supposed to be the one to teach her how to do the things that regular girls our age did, share the optimism I was supposed to have absorbed from growing up in a country-side surrounded by strawberry fields and avocado orchards. We would go swimming and eat pizza. I would rehabilitate her, strip the residue of the city from her pores and follicles, give her some kind of urban detox—except that I had just begun to discover how much I hated the things that were part of being a good girl, too.

Coquette and I were both new to being teenagers, new to having tits and periods and pubic hair, and we didn't understand quite how to deal with these things yet. She had turned 15 in May, and I was about to turn 14. We spent most of our time hanging out at my town's one little mall, or spread out on the couch in front of my parents' television. The TV sat in the middle of the living room with a giant statue of St. Francis on top of it—St. Francis being my mother's favorite, the patron saint of animals and innocent things.

At the mall, Coquette and I would stand around and lean against the wall by the drinking fountains; sometimes we smoked. We liked to hang over the second-floor railing, dangle our arms and legs over the edge like it was posted not to do. Sometimes, we'd congregate at the escalator, us and a bunch of other girls. We'd sip warm lemonades and eat our greasy corn dogs from Hot Dog on a Stick and talk about boys. We could spend hours there doing nothing, just hanging out. My cousin liked going to Sears because they sold khakis really cheap; she was a *chola* and they were part of a uniform she had pledged her loyalty to. It announced her origin and allegiance, something her purple sweatshirts, Nikes, and gold jewelry—the personalized necklace that spelled out "Coquette" in fancy cursive writing—were all part of.

She'd buy her khakis in size XL and then take them home to be washed, to shrink them down and soften them a bit. She'd tear off the tags and then lay the khakis out on the ironing board to be starched. She ruined my mom's ironing board that summer with all her starch and incessant ironing, but she needed creases running up the length of her pant legs. She'd stand at the board, a determined look on her face, mechanically but lovingly adorning her pants with straight, disciplined lines. She ironed everything: her sweatshirts, her socks. She even ironed creases into her underwear. She always wore baggy purple fleece sweatshirts, even on the hottest days; she'd prefer to sweat rather than relinquish any part of the ghetto uniform. She wore ankle socks with little balls that peeked out from under the backs of her pant legs and that bounced as she walked.

Her face and hair underwent a set of rituals, too. Before we could go out, she'd stand in the bathroom ratting her hair, spraying half a can of Aqua Net onto it to hold it in place, and then she'd pluck all of her eyebrow hair. She substituted eyeliner for lip liner and drew herself big, mean Mexican lips that made me jealous because I wasn't allowed to wear makeup until I turned sixteen. Her penciled-in eyebrows were unnaturally thin and arced and gave her a permanent look of angry surprise. I'd sit on the toilet seat watching her, and—perhaps sensing my latent capacity for being bad—she'd tease me, ask if there were any parties, anything to do, anywhere we could go to get fucked up. She'd say, "*Órale* cuz, there's got to be something to do. Call up one of your friends and hook us up." I'd get embarrassed and tell her not to worry, that we'd find something, some trouble to get into by the end of summer. Coquette would say, "I don't give a fuck if this is a small town. Even a small town's got trouble." Then she'd smile. I'd smile back.

Everyone thought that by putting her with me, her wicked, wicked, ways would change. Without Grape Street, her incubator would be gone, and her hardened mane of hair would melt away, as would the eyeliner and the purple lipstick, leaving the naked face of a girl underneath that everyone would recognize from a long time ago. I could fix her, reattach the hymen that had been busted over and over by the smog and the tears and the old *cholos*. But I couldn't do that, and I didn't want to. We were cousins, *primas*, and she was showing me what it meant to be dirty and bruised. You could see it on her face. And I liked it.

Sweetie, Darling

Kathleen Collins

I sharply remember that hot summer day in 1994. Having just finished graduate school, I was settling numbly into my first real job working as an administrator at a college near Boston. I was a nascent professional, saddled with new responsibilities and restrictions, but already tired of acting how I knew I should and ready to give my tired superego a break. That particular day, when lunch hour arrived, two female coworkers told me they were going home to watch a tape of the British sitcom *Absolutely Fabulous,* which had just aired in the U.S., and they invited me to join them. They could barely contain their excitement.

As soon as the tape went in and I began to decipher the accents, I was hooked. The episode was partly about one of the characters being unable to find her office at a fashion magazine because it had been so long since she'd been to work. I thrilled to the concept. Likewise, I felt no shock at her comment, "One snap of my fingers and I can raise hemlines so high the whole world's your gynecologist." Instead, I experienced a release and the false optimism otherwise only achieved after exactly 1.5 glasses of red wine on an empty stomach. An hour later, the three of us headed back to our shabby offices repeating the episode's dialogue line for line, enlivened by the gut-aching laughs and feeling oddly empowered and freed by its middle-aged anti-heroines' strident, insouciant behavior. As the months went by, our shared naughtiness in sneaking away once a week to watch Eddy and Patsy's bad behavior somehow tightened our bond, too, in that secret-club way. The *AbFab* women were our foils. They were our two-martini lunch, our joint in the parking lot.

For those who've never caught the show, Patsy Stone and Edina Monsoon are two aging hipster forty-somethings leading hedonistic, narcissistic, depraved lives. In the mirror, they see themselves as smart and cutting-edge, but to others they appear foolishly anachronistic and gaudy. Patsy is an Ivana Trump doppelgänger sporting a pile of dyed-blond hair, and Edina excels in wearing the hottest designers' styles to clownish effect. They numb their despair with alcohol and drugs and fend off their fear of aging with ridiculous clothing—and their fear of the world with biting sarcasm and self-absorption.

Eddy and Patsy have been friends since girlhood. There are flash-backs to their school days—Eddy and Patsy slumping against the wall out-side the principal's office, busted for smoking or having sex or some such—and to their wild, orgiastic, free-love times before Eddy begrudgingly (or mistakenly) became a parent. But the wild times resumed and flour-ished despite their adult responsibilities, to which neither pays any heed. Edina runs her own PR agency, where she represents a few unfor-tunate B-list celebs, and Patsy is on the payroll of a nameless fashion mag-azine, where she makes an appearance about once a year. However, their true vocation is clearly a never-ending mission to avoid the reality of the present. Eddy's bookish and long-suffering daughter, Saffron (Saffy), and doddering mother are the victims of relentless vitriol and abuse from Patsy and Edina. Eddy is a terrible mother and daughter, and she and Patsy offend and defend themselves against the plodding good sense of these two from the outer generations.

AbFab owes much to the classic female-buddy show, where nutty women find themselves in all sorts of pickles they can't get out of. Mary and Rhoda or Laverne and Shirley they are not, however. While Mary and Rhoda portrayed independent women in an intimate friendship—breaking boundaries for women in 1970s television—they were nice to each other. Laverne and Shirley's wacky partnership presaged Patsy and Edina's; but Laverne and Shirley were good girls at heart, and their friendship was ultimately a vehicle for the laughs—more *Odd Couple* than *AbFab*.

Patsy and Edina have been referred to as the "dysfunctional Lucy and Ethel," which is like calling the Simpsons the dysfunctional Cleavers, so far are they beyond conventional propriety. They are narcissistic, mean-spirited, and selfish, and they edge dangerously close to behaving sociopathically. In one episode, Patsy burns Saffy's arm with a cigarette just for the hell of it. In another, Eddy justifies her collection of Ethiopian bowls by pointing out to her daughter that, after all, "They've got nothing to put in them." Eddy and Patsy's shameless dipsomania and sharp tongues would impress even *Will & Grace*'s Karen Walker, who, one suspects, might be the only sitcom character able to give the two of them a run for their money. Like Karen, they have no sense of family, are ineffectual employees, and freely abuse substances. They are not always even the best of friends—they use each other, albeit without duplicity. Patsy, for instance, urges Eddy to get her navel pierced so she can see how much it hurts.

So why would anyone want to watch social miscreants make fools of themselves? For those of us who can stomach such cruelty and overwrought caricatures, Patsy and Eddy allow us the luxury and distance of vicariously lashing out at family and society, all the while remaining secure in our well-maintained scruples and manners. Patsy and Eddy's hyperactive ids and tell-it-like-it-is demeanor stirred something equally primal in my friends and me. Who among us does not wish for at least one day of such filter-free self-expression?

But the crux of the show is about something less evident. The comedy might come from Patsy and Eddy's debauched behavior, but it's really about the enduring friendship between them. If *Absolutely Fabulous* were about just one insanely self-indulgent lush, it might still be funny, but it would be fundamentally pathetic. Eddy and Patsy are, however, an ironically heartwarming team; they can count on each other, and they validate one another's horridness. When there are two of you, it's not an attitude problem—it's a lifestyle. Patsy and Eddy only have each other all along, and they know it—making their bond all the more vulnerable and precious.

Despite the over-the-topness of Edina and Patsy's behavior, my friends and I found their situation paradoxically and bracingly real. The show helped alleviate the postgraduate anxieties that pushed us together in an unspoken neediness: What if I don't find fulfilling work? Can I be myself as a grown-up? Will I be alone in life? During that time of uncertainty, Patsy and Eddy allowed us to laugh off those anxieties and even offer what seemed, for 40 minutes at a time, a possible safety net: If all goes horribly wrong, we will still have each other, and together we can enjoy the squalor of a failed middle age.

In contrast, it's interesting that *Friends*—which debuted the same year that *AbFab* came to the U.S.—felt too fantastical to reflect my generation's concerns, despite its semi-realistic twenty-something themes. Their apartments were too big, they never seemed to work, and they had good hair, all of which helped make the show addictive in its own right. When they slipped into socially unacceptable behavior, the plot would revolve around their subsequent embarrassment. Rachel, Monica, and Phoebe each had their own sets of problems and helped each other through indecision and insecurities, at times in touching ways. Nevertheless, the overall niceness of the women—not to mention the glib sitcom plotting—took any edge off the downsides of career angst, single parenthood, infertility, and divorce. There was never any question that the friends would ultimately find their way to happy, well-adjusted adult lives.

In some ways, the *Sex and the City* vision of friendship is closer to *AbFab*'s: These women were out to enjoy themselves—and in one another's company at least, they certainly did not hold their tongues. When I discovered the show, it was like an absolution. My friends and I had entered our 30s. We were finding actual wrinkles, ending long-term relationships we had thought would last, and felt our first suspect breast lumps. Except for the heels and hair, frequent sex with a variety of partners, great clothes, and high-paying jobs, the show was like looking in a mirror. These women were not only my age (which for once was explicit), they were also having the exact discussions my friends and I were.

But Carrie and company confronted the hard questions that a sitcom like *AbFab* can only allude to. After an episode of *Sex and the City,* my friends and I would chew on themes of loyalty, self-esteem, and betrayal—sometimes for days—in earnest. Couched in a highly palatable fantasy, the show brought our real-life issues to television. We hoped our mothers and boyfriends would watch so they could hear incisive Carrie explain what the trouble was, so we could say, "See? It's not just me!"

Still, *Sex and the City*—laden though it was with pathos and perfectly crafted, humorous sentimentality—was often too much like real life to offer true respite. It dealt with cancer, infertility, loneliness, and divorce, at times rendering it woefully heavy, though the show did end with a happy coupling for all, a baby for those who wanted one, and—most importantly—all the characters together in New York.

AbFab, as of this writing, is still with us, and audiences are never sure whether more seasons are on the horizon. So not only was *Sex and the City* unable to nudge out *AbFab*'s position in our hearts, but *AbFab* continues to be just as relevant in our 30s as it was in our 20s—and it remains to be seen how we'll perceive it in our 40s. While watching it, my friends and I are suspended in our alternate free-will universe, where, if those real-life dilemmas do crop up, Patsy and Eddy drink them away for us.

Unlike *Sex and the City* and *Friends, AbFab* can't come out and boast about how sustaining its central relationship really is without losing the power of its perverse comedy. The subject of friendship, while at the heart of the show, is read as subtext, obliquely referenced, never directly acknowledged. It's left to viewers to make assessments or comparisons to their own relationships.

Still, we take comfort in their insanely constant companionship, a given in that they both know they'll do everything together. Patsy and Edina ostensibly function as one another's life partners, family, and memories. They argue, attack, compromise, whine, and relent—like spouses, like sisters, like the best friends that they are—but there is no doubt that each is the other's lifeline, and they are committed to one another. Unlike the *Sex and the City* women (and my friends and me), who led their own healthily separate lives—off to work, dating, individual vacations—Patsy and Eddy see each other practically all day every day, so that each aspect of their lives merges into one life. They appear to take each other for granted but are nonetheless inseparable.

While theirs is, at least superficially, a dysfunctional arrangement, the idea of it assuages the worries my female friends and I harbor about growing old alone. Eddy and Patsy are essentially allies in a world that has become incomprehensible and frightening to them. Life is unfair, they can't count on men, they're angry at the aging process, but their miserable selves love the other's company. Too proud to admit their terror, they channel it into emotional toughness and disdain for everyone who is not a celebrity or at least rich and thin.

Yet the alliance does provide them with actual courage. In one late episode, just before the end of what was thought to be the last season, Patsy pleads earnestly with Eddy, "Don't ever make me a cup of tea." In other words, don't let me get old and become one of those boring old pathetic hags. Save me, protect me. This is what they have been doing for each other all along: holding each other up, perpetuating the charade that time is not passing, and thereby protecting each other from isolation and loneliness. They have found the perfect niche for their codependence, where they can function best.

Patsy and Edina's relationship spans most of their lives—including an imagined future together as senior citizens. This struck a chord with my friends and me, as it probably did for the legions of women who vow to be there for each other when husbands are long gone or if they never "achieve" couplehood with a romantic partner. Prematurely bitter about men in our freshman year of college, my best friend and I began fantasizing, semi-jokingly, about living together when we were old and our husbands (yet to be designated) were dead or otherwise absent. We read about the Boston marriages of the nineteenth century and thought we might like to live like that.

As we got older and men came in and out of our lives, we thought maybe we wouldn't wait until we were old. We gleefully painted verbal pictures of our household, us in creative, satisfying careers, our multiracial, adopted children happily underfoot. This Plan B at times supplanted the assumed Plan A. Patsy and Eddy live a version of this, though apparently inadvertently, since they show no signs of having any plans whatsoever. In a flash-forward episode to when they are old together, they are still joined at the now-brittle hip, wreaking insanity with less ensuing damage. They shuffle into their shared home, agreeing contentedly that theirs is "not a bad life"—as Patsy's knickers fall down of their own accord.

Above all, Patsy and Eddy represent the desire to say and do what we want when we want, society be damned—yet to still have someone who loves and accepts us for our flagrant, wretched, real selves. If, as the saying goes, all you need in this world is one good friend, then Patsy and Eddy have all they need. They may not be role models in any usual sense, but they do provide an irresistible fantasy romp and a measure of assurance to women of all ages that some relationships, no matter how imperfect, do last.

Ariel & Me

by Ellen Forney

Secrets and Confidences

78

The Barbie Basement

Sara Bir

The overwhelming majority of my female friends had no childhood affinity for Barbie dolls. "Barbies didn't do anything—all you could do was dress them," they say now, dismissively. Then they tell some brief and very clichéd tale of chopping off Barbie's hair or tearing out Barbie's arms, and then change the subject.

But what can you say about a girl who had no use for Barbie? It's not the dolls themselves that are boring; they just sometimes find underappreciative owners. In the hands of the right person, much like a divining rod, Barbies can become incredibly powerful, and even empowering.

My Barbies, of course, were in the hands of the best person possible: me. I knew exactly what to do with them, as did my two best friends. From the middle of second grade to the end of fifth, Barbies ruled our universe, and we theirs. Great eras of humankind have come and gone, leaving their indelible marks: the Stone Age, the Bronze Age, the Barbie Age.

Unlike the other ages of man, the Barbie Age encompassed not an entire civilization, but only three little girls who grew up on the same street. A year stood between each of us: Sarah, the oldest; Erin, the middle; and me, the youngest. To ease confusion between Sarah and Sara—as well as to establish without a doubt that I was the youngest in the trio—I was referred to as Bir Baby, or, for short, just Bir. Erin was my best friend, whom I idolized because she was older. We often played together, silly made-up games like Cat & Dog and Robin Hood. Sarah lived next door to Erin, and they also did their own things together. Generally, all three of us convened only for Barbie purposes. Although we did go to the same school, we were in different grades and Girl Scout troops; we went to different churches; and our older siblings ran in different social circles. Eleven-inch fashion dolls were our strongest bond, and only with these leggy plastic blonds in hand did we stand on equal ground. Our Barbie intimacy did not make us immune from hierarchy, however, in or out of character. Erin, as the middle girl, was in the difficult position of relating to both Sarah and me equally; she was our link, and because of that, I was even more worshipful of Erin, and jealous and suspicious of Sarah. When I called someone to play Barbies, it was Erin, and the three of us would spend the night only at Erin's house.

We performed our rites of Barbie in Erin's basement, a drywalled and carpeted space that Erin's parents had initially conceived as a rec room. In the Barbie Basement, we were totally sheltered from aboveground realities of good grades, popularity, and the massive (two-year!) age difference between Sarah and me. In this context, we shared the same sensibilities. Most Barbie-afflicted little girls deferred to the toy section of the *Sears Christmas Wishbook* to dictate their mode of play. They coveted Mattel-made Barbie Dream Houses or Barbie Mansions, flimsy plastic trifles of brightly printed cardboard and snap-together filigree that we knew better than to bother with. It took the entire basement to contain our cavalcade of Barbie opulence— not merely a dream house or mansion but a Barbie Dream Compound. Converted bookshelves, inverted dining-room chairs, and customized fruit crates created a framework we filled with bits of Barbie furniture, purchased as well as improvised from jelly jars and romance paperbacks draped with fabric.

We took one part television, one part our real moms, one part storybook princess, and one part our own future selves to construct imperfectly perfect women. Not only were our Barbies the richest women in the world, they were also sisters and ex-princesses. Mirroring real life, Sarah's Barbie was the eldest, Erin's the middle, and mine the youngest. Through the manipulation of our collective surnames, we crafted the Suerkwickbir dynasty from thin air.

Our princess sisters had renounced their royal affiliations with the Suerkwickbir dynasty in order to marry three Ken-doll brothers of low social standing. Despite having disposed of their glamorous regal lifestyles for the noble aspirations of true love and poverty, our girls' tenacity and determination motivated them to claw their way up the ladder of success at an unprecedented rate, the acute investment acumen of the self-starter Suerkwickbir sisters eclipsing the minuscule business know-how of their gorgeous husbands.

Our Barbies were the antithesis of the placid teenage persona Mattel had originally conceived. In their mid-forties—dynamic and shrewd and delightfully bitchy—our girls had stay-at-home husbands, grown children and grandchildren, and Fortune 500 businesses. They were career women and sex fiends, internationally famous, and always well costumed.

Our afternoons ran like proto–*Sex and the City* episodes. Erin's Barbie, a high-end fashion designer, stood at the helm of Barbie Designs, had power lunches with Oscar de la Renta, and had a deep-seated rivalry with Calvin Klein. Sarah's, a veterinarian who conducted genetic-modification experiments on farm animals, made use of Sarah's collection of Breyer horses, thoroughbreds that populated the Barbie stables.

My Barbie was an investment banker, head of Barbie International Corp. I didn't even know what an investment banker did—I still don't—but I perceived bankers as very, very powerful, and nothing less would do for my girl. As embodied by my all-time favorite Barbie doll, Day to Night Barbie, she dressed in a pink power suit that instantly converted—with the flip of a reversible skirt—into snazzy eveningwear. She had a pink briefcase, little pink-and-white oxford high heels, and a boxy white hat. Under the influence of Cybill Shepherd's character on *Moonlighting,* I named my girl Maddie Barbie. She talked back a lot—to her husband, to clients, to deliverymen, to servants, to her arch-nemesis, Alvin Klein. A very tanned Malibu Barbie from the late '70s assumed the role of Maddie's secretary. Her name was Charlene. She talked like a cross between a valley girl and a Long Islander and was always misplacing important papers.

There were always castoff, outdated Barbie dolls to assume the roles of secondary characters—maids, daughters—but Ken dolls were in short supply. We only had three, just enough to serve as husbands. Like ventriloquist's dummies, they spoke in pained, pinched voices we called the "Ken voice." Being young girls, it was our best stab at replicating a grown man's deep tones. The Kens' basic function was twofold: to get in the way and bungle things so that we—their wives—could reprimand them, and to supply physical affection. Our sexual education ran in tandem with our Barbie dramas. Our girls, after all, had prolific sexual appetites; they would spend great energy chasing their tired-out husbands all over their vast estates for a lay. Whenever they felt romantic, the Barbies would saucily coo to the Kens, "Hey, wanna do the bills?"—their secret code for hot action. They never had sex in bed, because finding more exotic locations provided endless plot variations. Our interpretation of sex was to get Ken and Barbie naked, facing each other in a plastic embrace. Then we'd wrap them up in the Barbie Bedroom Suite bedspread and have them roll enthusiastically all over the floor as we made exaggerated kissing sounds. Usually all of this was set to the smooth, romantic jams on Whitney Houston's debut album, a choice record for "doing the bills" to.

Sometimes we got very creative. Every time some new bit of information came to light—blow jobs, orgies, usually through the elder wisdom of Sarah—we'd incorporate it into our ongoing Barbie soap opera. How else were we supposed to learn about things like that? Our Barbies' naughty teenage daughters got pregnant and had to give their babies up for adoption. Our Barbies' maids and a duo of Strawberry Short-cake Purple Pie Men (because of the scarcity of Ken dolls) experimented with group sex. The Barbie sisters, feeling frisky one night around Halloween, traded heads and had sex with each other's husbands.

Frequently we'd spend the night at Erin's house and have an all-night Barbie marathon, where our most intricate and inspired story arcs came to fruition. We'd arrive just after school—where we never spent time together, not even during recess—on Friday, spend a few hours in the Barbie Basement, stay for dinner, run back to our houses to grab overnight bags, play Barbies until eleven P.M., have chocolate milk and marshmallow Pinwheel cookies, play Barbies until our eyes were rimmed with red, and collapse into our sleeping bags sometime after one in the morning.

In the Barbie Basement, we were not friends, but sisters; not girls, but women. We didn't play; we became. We practiced being adults. Our own lives were innocent and carefree, but our Barbies had stressful, jet-setting lives filled with demands: kids, husbands, jobs, fame, unfathomable wealth.

Pretending, though, can only carry you so far. Being the oldest, Sarah was the first to go. Around sixth grade, mere playacting no longer satisfied her maturing tastes. Instead of making Barbie kiss Ken, she was now making out with real boys herself. Soon Erin, propelled by her admiration of Sarah's newfound worldliness, was more inclined to gossip with Sarah's older friends than to play dolls with me. In the glimmer of their daughter's puberty, Erin's parents saw their chance to get that rec room installed at long last. Right after my fifth-grade year came to a close, the Barbie Basement was dismantled.

I went into withdrawal. Sixth grade was awful, full of young bodies beginning to change and young social ambitions beginning to flower. Erin and Sarah were preoccupied with the preteen complexities of shaking off unpopular (read: younger) company and snaring the attentions of living (not plastic) boys. As the youngest and a perpetually late bloomer to begin with, I couldn't catch up fast enough. My fictional self could move much more freely through fantasy than I could through real-life school social structures.

Erin and I continued to spend time alone together; sometimes Sarah would join us. As a threesome, we now took trips to the mall, and at our sleepovers, we passed the hours watching the Brat Packers couple and uncouple on a worn-out videocassette of *St. Elmo's Fire* rather than coupling our own Barbies, as we would have done just a year before. Sometimes we'd go toilet-paper Bill Brodie's house. Having older friends to guide me through the subtleties of petty vandalism was thrilling at the time, though it didn't ring with the same character-building power that the Barbie Basement had given us.

Halfway through high school, Sarah moved to Florida while in the middle of a rebellious sexual phase wherein she had already bedded more boys than I, at thirteen, had ever had crushes on. She eventually calmed down, became a nurse, and married a nice man.

The last time I saw her was at Erin's wedding. Erin—whose parents still live on the same street as mine—and I remain close. I know how she would react to events or situations—plagues of locusts, corporate takeovers, volcano explosions—that may never happen to her, because I've seen Erin's Barbie react to those very events. We acted them out together with our girls. Erin can predict how my as-yet-unscheduled wedding will play out because she witnessed Maddie and her Ken doll renew their wedding vows about a thousand times. We see each other maybe once a year, and speak on the phone maybe twice; our shared past is strong enough that we can still instantly fall into our former easygoing chatter. Erin today reminds me of her Barbie alter ego, only instead of designing fashions she teaches third grade—but she does so with an iron fist, just as she presides over her household and her very wonderful real-life husband.

The '80s were our Golden Age of Barbie. At the time, the Barbie jingle went "We girls can do anything, right, Barbie?" We took this to heart, using our Barbies as mouthpieces for the issues, concerns, and ideas that passed through our young lives.

Erin and I shudder to see the state of Barbies today. Mattel went from the dynamic Barbie for President Barbie and Astronaut Barbie to SpongeBob SquarePants Barbie and Totally Hair Barbie. The average American girl today stops playing with Barbies at age six. Think of everything those girls are missing out on—all of the Barbie corporate takeovers, the Barbie head exchanges, the orgies. Even a megaprecocious six-year-old can't play Barbies even halfway right, and that's all there is to it. All of these girls who abandon Barbie before their time are going to grow up with television and movies and bad teen magazines as their guide for the way the world works—but they are not going to have any practical experience. Mattel may have manufactured our Barbies, but it was Sarah, Erin, and I, and the interchange of our imaginations, who shaped what they became and symbolized for us. And that exchange helped shape us, too: I'll never be ashamed to say that.

Ascending Borders

Marisa Handler

I disliked Ronit the moment I met her. She was presumptuous, full of herself, garrulous. She stepped into my limelight far too frequently. We lived in the same dorm, and no matter what the social circumstance, Ronit would enter the room apparently assuming that everyone had been hanging out wondering when she'd arrive to leap in and dominate the conversation. I was mildly flabbergasted to find that others seemed to tolerate—even enjoy—her volleys of enthusiasm. She struck me as loud, impossibly self-important; she held firm convictions about everything under the sun and reliably offered seven opinions for every topic of conversation.

It was our freshman year in college, that intense, squalling infancy of adult life. I had defied my parents and abandoned the manifold torments of Los Angeles (or, more precisely, high school in the San Fernando Valley) for Berkeley's green grasses, and I was high on every bit of it: the freedom, the books, the boys, and of course—in liberal doses—the unquestionably superior weed. I was content with my three roommates, even with us sharing a twelve-by-twelve-foot room.

At that sunny moment, mere days into first semester, I adored unabashedly all that comprised my new unfettered life—a happiness dented only by Ronit. In the nirvana of my hard-won freedom, I didn't feel like compromising one bit: I would be as wild and free, and as strident and obnoxious, as I pleased. It wasn't for naught that I'd escaped both having to endlessly babysit my younger brother and endure the firm discipline of my South African parents. Ronit rubbed me the wrong way precisely because she behaved so much like me—and was unafraid to challenge me. Not only did she echo the rather less subtle strains of my own carefully cultivated persona, but she provided some real competition. With Ronit around, I wasn't always right.

Of course, Ronit disliked me in turn. She thought me—me!—arrogant. And self-aggrandizing. And uncompromising. She wasn't altogether wrong, in hindsight, and these grievances were suspiciously similar to my own. Yet out of some generous impulse, or perhaps simply the reflexive conditioning of years of Hebrew-school droning on *tzedakah* (charity), she invited me to join her family for Rosh Hashanah. I was rather taken aback by the invitation, but I accepted. I knew no other Jews in Berkeley, and I wasn't quite far enough from home to escape my parents' edicts, not to mention the occasionally credible Eye of God.

Ronit's parents lived in Palo Alto, which I would soon discover to be a teeming hive of a couple thousand equally loud and opinionated Israeli expatriates. The ride there did not bode well: Ronit and some other Israeli yapped away in Hebrew in the front, as I contemplated the potential horrors of an entire weekend in the company of this obnoxious young woman. She had invited me, no doubt, merely to torment me by communicating with everyone else—presumably about me—in a language I could not understand. Yet at some point over those two days, something in each of us relaxed. I remember walking back together from a service, vigorously debating the relative merits of a certain water polo player's broad chest versus his vacuous brain, and sliding with sudden ease into a sensitive discussion of how it felt to be an immigrant in this country. Out of nowhere, our conversation took on the kind of erratic fluidity that characterizes deeply familiar, comfortable relationships. I remember thinking, Huh, she's actually not that bad. Pretty funny. No filter—she just says exactly what she thinks. That's kind of cool. What a character.

And that was it. We fell madly, deeply, in love.

I had never had a best friend before. Nor had I had an all-consuming romantic relationship. Ronit and I were not that: If there were any sexual undertones, we were far too naive and thoroughly programmed to act on them. But in every other way, our relationship resembled that ineffable bond to which poets scribe flowery odes and crooners sing eternal. What joy! To have all I desired in one beloved soul, in one Best Friend. Together we laughed uproariously, drank voraciously, studied assiduously, and fought loudly—I remember one tempest in our dorm elevator, when fellow riders watched bemused as Ronit stormed out in a rage on the sixth floor, then sprinted down, repentant, to meet me as we paused on the third. Our separate, tentative sexual exploits came nothing close to the passion, vigor, and downright mutual adulation of our relationship. We wrote birthday cards proclaiming our devotion to each other, laying out the bare bones of what was profoundly beloved in each. We sang together. We camped together. When my grandmother died, far away and deeply missed in South Africa, we mourned together. And naturally we had our daily routine: classes, then back to the dorm, a hit or two from a shared bowl, off to dinner (we attacked the bland smorgasbord of the dining commons with a vengeance, then sat and snorted at each other in a corner), over to the library or a café to study, then home to a goodnight bowl. Ah, it was beautiful.

And it was tragic. We both knew it was tragic, because Ronit had decided before even beginning studies at Berkeley that she would make *aliyah* after her first year of college. Despite my best efforts—and I wielded considerable influence over the girl—she would not change her mind.

Aliyah: from the Hebrew verb *la'alot,* to rise or ascend. To make *aliyah:* to return to the homeland, or, in the spiritual or biblical sense, to ascend to a higher plane. Ronit had left Israel with her family at age seven, but she'd been raised drenched in the culture, in the colorful mythology and ancient dream of a Jewish homeland. Well before I strolled onto the scene, Ronit had determined to make her life in Israel. She only enrolled at Cal for a year because it made one a better candidate for life in Israel—for a slated army stint and then entry into university.

Not that I didn't understand. My family had been thoroughly entrenched within the Capetonian Jewish community. After emigrating to the U.S., we had floundered trying to find community here, but I'd finally located some of my identity within the summer camps of Habonim Dror, a Zionist socialist youth movement. Habonim was a radical bastion for me, far removed from the mainstream world of my high school. I had never visited Israel—yet in my head its name rang with iridescent clarity: It embodied strength, divine affirmation, the vindication of the lost dreams of countless persecuted Jews for more than two thousand years. I understood why Ronit wanted to return. I had eagerly swallowed much of the same lovely, numinous propaganda.

We parted with tears and endearments. I really had no idea how I could possibly enjoy life without her. For the first chunk of my sophomore year, I missed Ronit constantly and violently. We called and wrote often. She enrolled in the army; I immersed myself in the not-unpleasant routine of academic work and parties. Ronit went home to a kibbutz on the weekend; I moved into the co-op system with close friends and grew closer to them. Ronit was nominated to be an officer (I was mildly stunned at the thought of Ronit the Stoner commanding real soldiers in a real army); I applied for and was selected to be conflict mediator for the Berkeley co-ops. Ronit sobbed to me over the phone: The women in the army gossiped constantly about her behind her back; the men she had crushes on broke her heart. Some of my friends started talking about spending their junior years abroad; I signed up for the Jerusalem program.

There was an exquisite thrill to first setting foot in Israel. Between the varied lore I'd absorbed from synagogue, Hebrew school, and a Zionist youth movement, Israel had become totemic. I was almost surprised it existed at all, that it wasn't merely a space of hallowed imagination. I recalled the hundreds of thousands of Jews who'd landed here from all over the world, from exile and deprivation and horrendous persecution. I refrained from kissing the ground, but every inch of those red hills, as we rode from Tel Aviv to Jerusalem in the descending twilight, shone holy.

There was a group of us from the University of California program, and we spent most of that first gorgeous summer learning Hebrew in Haifa. At the close of summer, we went straight to the Hebrew University of Jerusalem, where we would spend the rest of the year. My first day there, Bibi Netanyahu, prime minister at the time, opened tunnels in the Old City that technically were not Jewish property; they were part of the Arab quarter. Arabs all over the city responded with riots and stone-throwing. I was living in a tiny outpost of West Jerusalem (Jewish) surrounded by East Jerusalem (Arab). I was instructed not to leave the dorm and spent the next couple of days hiding out, terrified.

In 1996, bombings did occur, but relatively rarely. I was just as scared of accidentally walking through an Orthodox Jewish neighborhood in a short skirt—I'd surely be stoned and abused for indecency. Nonetheless, this kind of insecurity was new to me, and it took me a while to get used to sharing the bus with uniformed soldiers. They were invariably young and passed out from exhaustion, their M-16s propped casually against a window.

I adjusted slowly to this new environment, and Ronit and I spoke frequently on the phone, both eagerly anticipating seeing each other again. She was in the army, and could only leave her base every fortnight. The next time she had a break, I went to visit her on her kibbutz, Gesher Haziv. Our reunion was blissful and we celebrated fittingly. We got ragingly drunk at the kibbutz pub, then bopped around raucously to the Jackson Five and giggled at the few startled regulars. We waltzed out arm in arm, Ronit shrieking nonsense at the geese roosting just outside.

But our reunion had its share of difficulties, too. Ronit had made such efforts—and sacrifices—to adjust to her new life that she had some real resistance to opening up to me again. She was, at times, closed to the point of hostility, and this was very painful. When we hung out with her Israeli friends, she was often dismissive of me. When we argued, she obviously considered my opinions merely the misguided naivete of an indulged, soft American. Ronit seemed intent on proving how much she had changed, how independent of me she had become. I had the disturbing impression that she felt I was a remnant of her old self, a self she no longer respected, and thus my presence inspired resentment. It took us a while to work through the ways we'd both changed, to connect properly. But finally we broke through: I distinctly remember one conversation that took place as we floated far out in the mellow waters of the Mediterranean, on a beach in the north near Gesher Haziv. It was Ronit's idea to seal our renewed best friendship by exchanging bikini tops. Hers was padded, and somehow a pad worked itself loose in the transfer. I was laughing so hard that there was no way to catch it. Ronit jokingly berated me the entire way back, in both Hebrew and English, as I made clumsy attempts to swim through my hysteria. It was so good to be together again.

My year in Israel was transformative. As a Jew, I'd always been in the minority, no matter where I'd lived. In Israel, I found myself among an extended community that felt profoundly familiar, despite my never having set foot on the continent before. Initially, I found Israelis to be disconcertingly aggressive—communication was curt, pared clean of any niceties—but I adopted a similarly tough demeanor and quickly discovered the gristly goodwill lurking beneath the veneer. I learned Hebrew and insisted that the stubborn natives speak it with me. I visited the Old City regularly and reveled in the ancient history held by their walls.

Yet my year there was by no means easy. Israel is a deeply divided country in a multitude of ways: religious versus secular; Ashkenazi versus Sephardic Jew; second or third generation versus immigrant; Avodah (Labor) versus the conservative Likud. (In a country that has been at war for virtually its entire existence, politics matter.) And, of course, Jew versus Arab. Jerusalem is emblematic of these rifts, as it is essentially two cities. I gradually realized that leaving West Jerusalem required an active effort. No city buses ran through East Jerusalem, and we were warned on our program not to stray. Contact with Arabs was largely restricted to my frequent trips to the Old City. The *shuk,* or market, in the Arab Quarter rapidly became my favorite place in town. It was saturated with piquant scents and ornately exotic tidbits, and I adored haggling with the amiable, teasing merchants.

The rest of my contact with Arabs was with those in service positions: taxi drivers, janitors, and vendors. I worked a brief stint as a waitress at a café on BenYehuda, an outdoor mall in downtown Jerusalem. The other waitresses were all Israeli Jews; the busboys were Arabs. The waitresses treated the busboys like dirt, regularly flinging abuse at them throughout the day. I was shocked. It was disturbingly reminiscent of the sociopolitics I'd experienced as a child in apartheid South Africa.

It also proved frustratingly difficult to escape my program, which felt like an island of self-involved North Americans in the middle of Israel. Very few of my peers were politically concerned or involved. I became somewhat politically active, serving as the "foreign school representative" to Ofek, the student Avodah party. But while I remained informed and dutifully despised the reactionary Netanyahu, I found it hard to be active when my views were routinely dismissed as the ill-begotten naivete of a foreigner—never mind the large and active native Israeli peace contingency. I continued to rant when politics came up, but mostly I focused on my studies and social life. As I recall, though Ronit and I only lived a couple of hours away from each other by bus, and saw one another fairly frequently during the course of that year, we didn't discuss politics much. And when we did, we seldom disagreed.

It wasn't until after I returned to the U.S. that I became truly active. When I graduated, it felt like being pushed callously out of a delightfully warm womb. I dabbled in various fields, trying to figure out just what exactly I wanted to do when I grew up. Many of my explorations fell within the Jewish community: coordinator of a Jewish Community Center program for teens, Hebrew-school teacher. In the meantime, as events in the Middle East worsened, I felt increasingly called upon to speak my conscience. It seemed obvious: Palestine is a nation of people who are being denied a homeland, just as the Jews had been for so long. Except that in this case, it was my people doing the denying. As a Jew, I am a citizen of Israel; as a citizen who loves her country, I see it as my duty to criticize the Israeli government when it is doing something destructive not only to the notion of peace in the Middle East, but also to an Israeli democracy. The Occupation—yes, capital O—is an occupation, for god's sake. The very word connotes oppression. To my dismay, almost every otherwise "progressive" Jew I met disagreed. And vehemently.

I wasn't sure what to do, how to express my frustration, my dissent. Where were others like me? Then I began attending rallies. I discovered direct action and began organizing. In May 2001, I participated in a lockdown at the Oakland Federal Building, calling on the federal government to stop sending money for weapons to Israel. I sang, I made speeches, and I left thoroughly exhilarated. I accepted a job as the national organizer of the Tikkun Community and began traipsing around the country organizing bands of fellow dissenters.

Ronit visited a couple of times in the years after I graduated. As the situation in Israel and Palestine deteriorated, her politics, like those of many Israelis, moved to the right. We began to clash. While Ronit sits somewhere on the Israeli left and has never voted for a Likud candidate, she also views as justified the actions that leaders like Ariel Sharon have taken in the name of security. Actions that I see as acutely reprehensible—bulldozing houses and olive orchards, killing Palestinian civilians in crossfire aimed at terrorists, treating Palestinians like second-class citizens, even criminals, on their own land—are, to many Israelis, legitimate attempts to control terrorism. But to my mind, they simply sow more hatred and breed more terror among already desperate people. Peace among these neighbors cannot be fostered through tools of war.

But I don't live in Israel. I haven't had to live with the nightmare of suicide bombings. I'm not afraid when I go to my supermarket or to a club. And I can't say how this immense psychological burden would afflict me had I chosen to live there. Every Israeli knows someone whose life has been shattered by a bombing. When teenagers go out at night in Tel Aviv, they plan their route according to where it is least likely a suicide bomber would venture. Before Ronit's last visit, she begged me over the phone to plan a camping trip for us. "Somewhere green, for at least a couple of days," she said. I thought her yen to go camping stemmed from shared nostalgia for our lovely trips years earlier. But there was more to it. "I can't go camping here these days," she lamented. "I can't go to the Galil anymore. It isn't safe."

So I planned us a camping trip, to beautiful Big Basin Redwoods State Park in the hills of Santa Cruz. Then I awaited Ronit's arrival with some apprehension. I had not told her about my job at Tikkun. Whenever we'd discussed politics during her last visits, our conversations had reached unbreachable impasses. It had made us both angry and sad, and being that her visits were brief, these talks cast a significant pall over our time together. I knew she would thoroughly disapprove of my work, and I'd come to the unilateral conclusion that simply not discussing politics was the best way to preserve our friendship. That gem of an idea lasted about the first ten minutes of our drive to Big Basin. We spent the next forty-eight hours arguing.

Ronit took my work personally. In her eyes, I was single-handedly destroying the united Jewish front. She felt that my stance was the reason that Israel's political allies would desert her, and that everything I advocated was ruinous to the nation's security—in spite of the fact that, unlike many activists on the left, I firmly support the existence of a Jewish Israel. But I also see that Jews, because we are raised with the legacy of victimization and survival, are capable of denying our own long-cherished dream to another landless people. One of the consequences of abuse is that it replicates itself until it can be faced, in all its horror, with compassion.

While my understanding of all this lent me sufficient empathy to endure the torrents of anger hurled at me during various speaking tours, it got me nowhere with Ronit. We had known each other too long, and too deeply, to maintain any distance. Ronit simply couldn't understand why I would do work that, to her mind, unpinned the foundations of the only nation within which I was always guaranteed a home. She was outraged. She had made her life in Israel, and had made choices that allowed her to continue living there. In her eyes, I was a foolish idealist, and my commitment to this work pitted us in direct opposition to each other. I was stunned and dismayed by her inability to recognize the humanity of the Palestinians, by her easy dismissal of their suffering. We argued setting up the tent. We argued preparing our meals. I tried to ban the topic from our weekend, but it kept coming back. At one point, on a hike, we simply walked apart in silence. We had argued ourselves hoarse.

We spoke one more time, briefly. I called to say goodbye before she returned to Israel. Her mother, who called me a third daughter, picked up the phone. We exchanged the usual niceties in Hebrew, and then she began grilling me about Tikkun. I tried to be diplomatic. "No," she said. "You are wrong. You are doing terrible things. I hope your organization fails. I hope your magazine goes out of business."

"Tov," I said. "Okay. Is Ronit there?" She wished me love and handed over the phone.

It was a stilted conversation. I wished Ronit a safe journey, trying to inject a warmth into my voice that simply wouldn't come. She thanked me curtly. We listened to each other's breath over the phone, and hung up. There was nothing more to say.

Then came the e-mail wars. We wouldn't engage directly, but Ronit would send group e-mails out and include me on her list. One was an abominably racist joke about Palestinians. I replied to the entire list, wondering how any constructive resolution could ever come from such contempt. Ronit replied—again, to the entire list—and we proceeded to subject all the unfortunate recipients to a continuation of our argument. Another group e-mail she sent consisted of graphic photos from the latest suicide bombing. I did not reply.

These communications were very painful, yet I missed Ronit. I missed her and I was furious with her. And I was angry with myself, too. I went around preaching compassion and recognition of common humanity and mutual suffering—yet when it came down to it, I couldn't put my own theories into practice. How was I different from the "progressive" Jews whose politics veered abruptly right when it came to Israel? Or, for that matter, from anyone who holds comfortably liberal politics until the situation gets personal? How could I expect the conflict between Israelis and Palestinians to be overcome when I couldn't even maintain a friendship? We all have our breaking points, I reasoned, and perhaps this is mine. Perhaps from this I can learn compassion—not just for those who are suffering, but also for those who cannot give an inch, who hold their ideas so sacred that they become worth even more than human lives. Perhaps.

I thought a lot about calling Ronit. I thought about how terrible it would be if she got killed in a bombing and we had not spoken— no caring words exchanged, no attempt at reconciliation. But I couldn't call. I knew any conversation with Ronit would force me into defending my work yet again. Someone so close to me, so beloved and esteemed, felt that my work—to which I was fully committed, which was very demanding, and which was a perpetual emotional drain—was useless, actually destructive. This was sufficient ground not to call, I reasoned. And on a deeper level, it simply felt like calling would be giving in.

When I quit my job a year later, burned out and exhausted, I still didn't call, not wanting her to think she'd won. She was so far away anyway that it was almost possible to pretend it hadn't happened. Her visit had been so infuriating that it felt easier to just not think about our breakdown or mourn our friendship.

Then I heard through a mutual friend that Ronit's boyfriend had moved out. This was the man she'd been planning to marry, the man she'd fantasized about since she was twelve—the one who'd buy her a big house and sire her five chirpy kids. I could only guess what she would be feeling. I called.

"Marisa?" She was surprised.

"Yes, it's me. I heard Yair moved out."

"He did. So?"

"So I was worried about you. Are you okay?"

She sighed, and started talking. She talked for a long time. She talked for so long that I got a little nervous about my phone bill. I told her I had quit my job. No comment. She talked about how difficult it was living there. I sympathized, and we spoke of the latest suicide bombing. Twenty dead, in Haifa.

"God, it's terrible," I said.

"Yes," she said. "Yes." We were silent a moment. Then she started talking again. Finally she paused. "You know, it's good that you called. I'm impressed with you."

"I'm glad I called, but I didn't call to impress you."

"I know. But it's . . . it's really good to speak with you."

"It's good to speak with you too, Ronit. I'm glad to hear you're doing okay."

She told me she was coming to visit again in December. "Maybe you can plan ahead so we can take a weekend out," she said.

"Okay," I said. "I'll do that."

We didn't allude to having another conversation, or speak about our lengthy silence. But this was enough, for now. Somewhere inside, I'd always known we'd come together again. It simply wasn't an option not to; I was deluding myself to think the break might be permanent. Our friendship has never been easy. It's always challenged us in ways that sometimes feel easier to simply avoid. But it's also one of the most honest and beautiful relationships I have known.

We will never live in the same country. As a sophomore in college, I wept at this realization. We can't raise our children together, or share the daily dramas of our lives as they unfold. We needed to grow, and we have grown apart. But this much, we can do.

When Mary Met Sally

Marrit Ingman

The note was characteristically terse. *I can't be there because I'm gone.*

Along with it she had left behind her Ethan Allen wingback chair and an ugly pink throw rug with a southwestern motif. Weeks later, high and clowning around with the video camera in preparation for my film-school matriculation, I would drop a lit cigarette on the rug and burn a hole in it—accidentally, though the tape shows a twenty-year-old me cackling gleefully and poking the scorch.

I'd invited Sally out for margaritas after work so we could talk about the night before, when I finally said what I'd been wanting to say. Her reaction—palms raised to back me off, *I can't handle this*—had been predictable. But I hadn't expected to come home to her empty room, our other housemate shooting me cautious sidelong glances from his doorway. Lesbian roommate drama had interrupted *Charles in Charge*.

It had been building to this point since she and I first met in the rank basement office of our campus newspaper. As copy editors, we sat around a scratched-up table with felt-tipped pens and piles of diskettes, transposing typos. Sally wrote the headlines; I redacted so furiously that freshman writers would call me at home to complain about the atmospheric prose snipped from their lacrosse stories or their passionate editorials about curb painting for the elderly. Inevitably we began amusing one another, usually at the expense of other staffers. (Our editor checked his bank balance compulsively; our managing editor twirled around campus in broomstick skirts belting selections from *Hair;* our layout artist wore knee-high moccasin boots and dealt us our pot.) We'd all stay buried underground together overnight each Wednesday, cropping pictures, gassing each other with fixative spray, and getting positively hammered on cowboy coffee and Lone Star Bock smuggled in through the back entrance. One of us would ferry the paste-ups to the printer before his or her 8 A.M. class.

Yet, even with the intensity of this regular time together, Sally remained mysterious and inaccessible. While struggling with a recalcitrant printer or waiting for photos from the darkroom, we'd realize she'd been missing for an indeterminate amount of time. Then she'd materialize in her felt beret and pea coat, roses in her cheeks. "I've been to the movies," she'd admit in her gravelly alto. She'd somehow manage to slip out to a late showing of a documentary about Noam Chomsky or a French parlor comedy at the Village—Austin's now-defunct arthouse cinema—while we were camped around *Beavis and Butthead* in the student lounge, playing Rochambeau for the next beer run and waiting for our editor to come back with the toner.

It was months before we even knew she smoked. We were huddled on the back stoop with the door propped open and our backs to the wind, puffing furiously and despairing of how to fill the hole in the entertainment pages since Carrot Top canceled. The door squeaked open, and we automatically scrambled to grab it, fearful of being locked out. But Sally stepped out of the darkness with a packet of

Sobranies, flicked a Zippo, and took a drag of noxious Russian tobacco. We hadn't known her to have any vices beyond a predilection for Nutter Butters and bouts of Yiddish affectations that belied her Amarillo origins. She shook off our stares with an exaggerated shrug.

"You *smoke?!*" blurted our pothead designer, pointing at her for emphasis.

"Yeah, well, there are a lot of things about me you don't know." Even that statement was unusually informative.

I learned more about her slowly as our friendship deepened. Once we all arrived at her apartment for a newspaper function to find that she had just shaved her head with clippers and a guard. We circled round to rub our hands over her fine blond stubble. "Yeah, well," she said, surveying us. "I'm a dyke." Not that we had ever suspected otherwise. But her admission ushered in a new era of trust, which we encouraged by dosing her with Anaprox—our analgesic of choice for cramps—and beer.

When she first moved in with me, I discovered that she was a gourmand. She had boxes of Chantal cookware and Mexican chocolate, and esoteric cookbooks. I'd awaken to find her at the stove, concocting borscht. She had a weird assortment of tapes: Julie London, Elvis Costello, opera, the Blind Boys of Alabama. She was a cellist and a former debutante, but I could tempt her with low culture. We'd meet on the couch for *Melrose Place;* during moments of erotic tension on-screen, we'd shout, "Pork! Pork!" at the television. We watched *Where in the World Is Carmen Sandiego?* religiously, and Sally filled out two sets of postcards for the home-viewer game—one entry for her and one for me. We sent them off, hoping to win a T-shirt. She was also addicted to *Search for Tomorrow* and loved to grill sandwiches in the Snackmaster. We'd watch gymnastics contests with the sound off; I'd substitute music from my collection during the floor exercises. Our favorite was the theme song from *Shaft.*

Before long we didn't need an excuse to sit on the couch together. We'd just end up sitting there when the day was over, and we'd say things about ourselves: My sister died when I was nine; Sally was afraid of clowns. She teased me about my last ex-boyfriend, a modelesque hipster who'd contracted shingles halfway through our insubstantial relationship and become sexually useless. She told me about her father, a prominent radiation oncologist who was, ironically, dying of cancer. She wanted to tell him she was gay but couldn't determine whether he'd be devastated by the news.

One evening when we had rented movies, I persuaded Sally to smoke some pot with me. I had to teach her how to hold the pipe and light it. She was a quick study, and before long, we were standing in the kitchen staring into a bowl of cold leftover macaroni and cheese.

"Is it working?" she asked me.

"Do you want to eat that?" It seemed like an appropriate criterion. She dug in with her fork.

"Let me see if your eyes are red." She put down her fork and looked over. "They're green," I said. It was an unthinking observation, but it stuck in the air for what seemed like a minute—and not just because we were high. Something in my addled brain went *sproing.* I didn't agonize about the implications. I didn't really question whether I was straight or gay. I just knew that I was falling in love with her.

She went away to Russia the following semester, and I spent the two days after her departure crying in bed. By then we'd had several third roommates come and go. The latest came in to my room and sat down on my bed. She stroked my hair and told me everything was going to be okay. I sat up. Then we had a very academic discussion.

"I don't think you're really in love with her," she said.

I sniffled. What was in doubt?

"I mean, she's your best friend and you miss her," she said. That was true. I nodded.

"You don't . . . I mean, you're not attracted to her *sexually,* right? You *admire* her, right?" It wasn't like that. I wasn't compelled to put my feelings in a centrifuge and separate the sexy stuff from the rest of my appreciation. I liked people with wonderful brains. Who wouldn't want to fuck somebody with a wonderful brain? I got up and made myself coffee and went back to school.

Periodically I would get a letter from what was then still the USSR. In her angular scrawl, Sally would ask about our cat and opine about conditions in Moscow. She would talk about places she was planning to visit; tell stories about eating in a Soviet cafeteria; describe her housemates, who were from various countries and on the same program as she was. One of her housemates was a Spanish woman; they were seeing each other.

I wrote a poem in reply and never sent it:

You Make Me Feel like a Heterosexual Poseur

You're a bunch of grapes.
You're a gin Gibson and I'm a margarita from a bucket with
    an Old Milwaukee back.
You're a temperamental 1966 Corvair and I'm a Gremlin.
You're Edith Piaf and I'm Nancy Sinatra.
You're Marlene Dietrich in silk pajamas with Sid Vicious hair.
(Sorry the red wouldn't come out.)
You're a goddess in chambray,
a bringer of homemade pesto and Lou Rawls,
a harbinger of final Jeopardy!,
protector of the Family Medical Leave Act,
and I'm a meddling mortal with a polyester fixation and
    instant, processed food.

I eat from cans. You scorn me!
I fall upon the thorns of life. I bleed!
You wake me in the morning with the sound of the blender.
    Gazpacho!
My life hasn't been the same without you and your VCR.

Secrets and Confidences

If you turned me loose in Whole Foods I'd scramble for an
        exit, knocking over displays of herbal menstrual reme-
        dies and variety trail mixes, and if you took me camp-
        ing I'd try to escape by hitching rides with truckers in
        air-conditioned cabs until I reached a hotel with cable
        and free local calls and a complimentary continental
        breakfast.

Then I'd eat the mint and put myself to bed in my climate-
        controlled fiberfill cavern, wearing the shirt you left
        behind in the dryer.

A phantom of you still hangs out in the house,
shouting at the TV ("Who is *Shostakovich,* you shit!")
bringing in the mail
wandering the halls with a green wool muffler and a
        vodka tonic
hair sticking up
occasionally bringing home rented movies.

Don't worry.
I won't make you into a parlor trick.
I won't make you do your Richard Attenborough impression.
I won't make you act like Christopher Walken in *The Dead Zone.*

And I don't want to freak you out
so I won't tell you anything you don't want to hear.
So don't read this, I guess.
I'm sorry.

    The indignities continued all spring. When she returned I met her
at the airport, but back at school, Sally began consorting with a mutual
friend of ours who was everything I wasn't. Emily was tall and outgoing

and athletic; I was short and sulky, and my idea of exercise was walking my library books to the circulation desk. Emily had healthy Frisbee-chasing dogs that rooted in your crotch and exhaled doggy breath in your face after they'd knocked you over; I had a fat, pampered tabby that would sit on your chest and lick your nose until it was scabby. Emily was a fully confirmed political lesbian; I was murky and ambiguous. Emily was involved in a long-term live-in relationship with another person; I was available and living under Sally's roof.

We would all do weird things socially in an attempt to be inclusive. We'd all pile into Sally's Bronco and go to the park, where the dogs would run around and terrify picnickers. Emily would make jokes and Sally would laugh, and Emily's partner would fume and I would silently ask the sky what I had done to deserve this ridiculous situation. Why couldn't the two of us live in a wood-frame bungalow with ferns on the porch and a lime-washed gourmet kitchen redolent with the smells of carrot muffins and passionate love? Failing that, why couldn't I have clearly delineated platonic friendships with fun girls who brought home Bacardi and fraternity men with promising futures? Why was I always stuck in between the various possibilities?

So I came home from work one evening and knocked on Sally's door. She didn't want to talk. Graduation was on the horizon; her father was hospitalized, and it looked like he wasn't going to hang on much longer. She was packing to go to Amarillo for a visit. Emily was coming by later. Sally's mouth was a tight, determined little line.

I took a walk to clear my head, and came home determined to speak my mind. I had been waiting a year. I needed her to know how I felt. So I charged back into the house, full of purpose.

Now Sally was in the living room, folding boxes. I opened my mouth and started to speak, but she raised her palms to stop me. "I know what you're about to say," she said. "And I can't handle this."

All night I listened to the sounds of Sally and Emily talking. The phone rang a few times, and I could hear packing tape rip. Then my alarm rang, and I got up to dress for the clerking job I'd taken to pay my rent through the summer. Before I left, I scribbled a note. *Don't leave angry. We can be friends. Let's meet for margaritas.* I taped it to the door of the room where Sally and Emily were sleeping.

I'd hoped she'd meet me for drinks later. But she couldn't be there because she was already gone.

Now here's the part where we flash forward ten years. I am sitting in my home office writing our story. Where once there would have been a housemate in the room across the hall from me, there is now a sleeping baby; my first son, eighteen months old. His father and I have been married for five years. He was the first person I dated after Sally left. We met in film school. Now he is a public-school teacher and I am a freelance writer. I work mainly as a critic, but sometimes I write about things that have happened to me: postpartum depression, corporate layoffs, falling in love with someone.

My son has just learned to call her name. He can't quite form the consonants, so he enunciates the syllables—emphatically. We have a board book that shows toddlers with all their family members. Two children are baking cookies with their aunt. "Like your Aunt Sally," I tell him.

"Aunt Sally," he replies, in his way.

Aunt Sally left for good the night after I tried to talk to her, and we didn't speak to one another for a couple of years. I still heard from her somehow. Once she sent me two Super-8 cameras, old family relics she thought I might be able to use. No note inside the parcel, just an Amarillo postmark. I had to hunt her down at home through her mom. Sally's father had just died. Our conversation was brief and terse but I managed to thank her.

That Christmas I received a package of fudge from Sally and Emily; they had moved to Atlanta together. E-mails began popping up in my in box: Sally telling me about a Babes in Toyland concert, Sally telling me about her new cat, Sally musing about the hot weather.

When Mary Met Sally

I can remember feeling elated by the sound of her voice in my mind every time I read my messages. What did this mean about our relationship? I began to scheme and wonder. My now-husband and I had just started dating, but I still hadn't quite given up on Sally. I'd catch myself fantasizing about her wanting me back. I'd check my messages between every class, waiting for her to say it: *I was wrong*. Then I realized I wasn't really listening to her. I was coddling myself with the idea of her friendship. My ego needed her to love me, to put herself out there the way I had. I needed her to reciprocate. I needed her, at least, to apologize, to express sorrow for me. But if we were really going to be friends, I had to accept her on her terms—not on mine.

As I was completing my thesis, Sally sent me an update—a new address, a new phone number back in Austin. By the time Sally came to our wedding reception a year later, she had become, of all things, a UNIX systems administrator. She was living by herself in a cute wood-frame bungalow with ferns and muffins. Emily was gone, but Sally didn't say where. Even now I don't know all the details. I'm not sure how to ask for them, or even if I want to know, and Sally doesn't bring it up. Which is typical—to this day, we've never specifically talked about what happened between then and now. I mean, she knows how I felt. She's as much as said "I know how you felt," but that's as far as it's ever gone, and we probably nodded and smiled and lit cigarettes and went back to watching *Queer Eye for the Straight Guy*.

I had primed my husband to meet her. I told him that she was one of my favorite people. She was smart and weird and introverted. She and I were born eight hours apart; we were astrologically identical. And I told him that I used to be in love with her. I had moved on from that to love her differently. I thought he would object to Sally, jealously. He didn't.

I arranged for us to sit together on the couch with red wine and low culture—*Showgirls,* which we watched drunkenly, howling. We each assigned ourselves a signature line of dialogue.

His: I'm erect. Why aren't you?
Hers: You look better than a ten-inch dick.
Mine: I have a problem with pussy.

When my son was born, Sally and my parents were the first visitors at the hospital. I was a little self-conscious about being naked and catheterized around her, but she seemed unruffled. ("I'm down with breast-feeding," she said.) When Will was fussy, she came over to help. She stayed with me during a full day of colic-related screaming. We took turns walking the baby and watching her *Buffy the Vampire Slayer* tapes.

She put Will in the baby sling and cracked wise. "Some folks call it a sling baby," she told me, affecting her best Karl Childers impression with her gravelly voice. "I call it a Kaiser baby."

Later that day, when the baby was finally asleep and I was getting ready for bed, the phone rang. It was Sally.

"I just wanted to let you know that I love you guys," she said. "And I'm really glad you have a baby."

I told her I loved her, too.

Rush

Mara Schwartz

Sorority life as seen in the movies: ivy-covered Victorians, girls in pretty pastel dresses holding lighted tapers, and square-jawed frat boys extending their hands and hearts. Don't forget the pillow fights conducted by white-panty-clad females (complete with strategically located peephole in wall), beer bongs, and "Louie, Louie," of course.

In reality, sorority life might not be quite as over-the-top as that (a good thing or a bummer, depending on your perspective), but for at least a century, the Greek system has been a tried-and-true way for women to meet other women and participate in both all-female and coed social events with people their own age at many North American colleges and universities. Of course, that's something lots of young women do via other channels, but sororities' selling point is that they don't just hook you up with other girls to hang out with: Once you go through the rush process and join, you're not merely garden-variety buddies or roommates, but lifelong sisters.

Much the way Holy Communion lays claim to turning bread into honest-to-Jesus flesh, sorority membership takes a gaggle of girls, most of whom have never previously laid eyes on each other, and pronounces them a big extended family. This is reinforced with lots of attendant familial terminology: Active members who assimilate newbies into the group through the pledging process are "pledge moms"; the older woman who lives in the house and runs things is the "house mother"; everyone's got a "big sister" and at least one "little sister."

As far as I was concerned when I was entering college, I had my own real-life family and didn't really need a new and improved one. I had an actual mom who was giving me all the momming I could stomach in the weeks before her only kid moved out of the house, and no blood-related sisters but enough female friends to keep me on the phone at all hours. (And, hey, a dad, too!) And I didn't really fit the sorority-girl stereotype—I was, and still am, really into nonmainstream music and record stores, and I've had friends describe me politely as "offbeat." To put it into a context roughly contemporaneous with my actual sorority life, my style was closer to Molly Ringwald in *Pretty in Pink* than Molly Ringwald in *The Breakfast Club.*

But I was heading off on my first venture ever out of the nest, living on campus and attending a major public university—let's call it RLU, for Really Large University—located about an hour from where I grew up. Because it was a good school and relatively close to home, I was embarking on my new college life with three of my closest high school girlfriends, and they all decided sorority life was for them. Having heard horror stories of how big and overwhelming going to RLU can be (completely untrue, by the way; it was really fun), and envisioning sitting alone in my dorm room while my only three friends headed out to amazing sorority parties without me, I figured I'd better join up as well. (I should have learned my lesson from the previous year's disastrous high school cheerleading-tryout incident, an enterprise upon which I embarked for the same reason; everyone made the squad but me—but I lived.)

Rush

As you've probably gathered, I rushed, and joined a sorority back in 1985. That was the year *Out of Africa* won Best Picture and "Careless Whisper" by Wham! was a hit, so please picture my experiences, which I am about to describe, with the '80s haze they deserve. Yes, that does mean Madonna-wannabe haircuts, armfuls of jelly bracelets, and a world in which pink and gray actually matched.

Rush—the notorious few days that stand between a regular college girl and her newfound family—varies slightly from school to school, but every rush aims to channel a motley crew of women into roughly homogeneous groups, so that women end up in houses with others who share complementary interests and values. Even though I rushed twenty years ago, the basics never really change: These tradition-based organizations are solid as rocks, their decade-spanning continuity the whole point of their existence. Just to be sure, I ran through the website for RLU sorority "recruitment" (they don't call it "rush" anymore, though I'm not sure what was wrong with that), and everything Greek-related appeared to be the exact same deal—though there are considerably fewer sororities on campus now. (I was pleased to see my house is still alive and kicking.)

Rush is an exhausting, often demoralizing, frequently bewildering process that involves several eight-hour days of forced smiling, hand-shaking, and nigh-impossible name-remembering that kicks off every morning in a mass frenzy. I had to be up and at 'em to claim my bids (invitations to that day's parties) at 8 A.M., which meant jostling for blow-drying space with hundreds of other rushees in the dorms at 6:30—which didn't usually result in anyone's best look. Then we'd all troop across RLU's massive campus in the late-summer heat to Sorority Row—a line of houses on the eastern border of RLU (the frat boys were housed in the west)—in nervous anticipation.

Most sorority houses look pretty much alike, especially when you're visiting about ten of them a day. The ones at RLU had neutrally painted walls and generic dentist-office couches, and the biggest variation among the women was their place on the geek-versus-cool spectrum depicted so nicely in *Revenge of the Nerds*. (This can be sussed out within five minutes of walking through the door, if a fellow rushee hasn't clued you in already.)

To help us keep them straight, RLU's Panhellenic Council (its official sorority-system governing board) designated part of the week as theme days, when the house would get decked out in various politically correct motifs—Roaring Twenties, *The Wizard of Oz,* cowgirls, and so on. (Apparently they don't do this at every school; friends who'd pledged at other universities look at me funny when I mention them.) Although I'd be wearing whatever dress or flouncy skirt I thought sorority girls wanted in their line of vision, the actual members were often dressed as a rag doll or hula girl, depending on the day. I'd converse with a member for a whopping five to ten minutes, and then the interviewing members would rotate around the room with square-dance precision, so that I'd meet three or four of the house's sisters per party before moving on to the next house—very similar to speed-dating.

There would also be a brief show put on by the members that the house reprised for each party, relating somewhat to the theme, and involving skits and the singing of cultlike songs—usually revamped versions of maudlin pop songs for that extra-creepy vibe—about how much they loved their sisters and how their house was the best. There were slide shows of fun-looking group activities, such as football games and formals. Everything was carefully monitored by the Panhellenic Council—including the type of beverage and snack that could be served up on each day, so as not to give any house a culinary advantage. The Panhellenic snack rules at RLU were downright draconian, to the point of farce: "plastic cup of water with one garnish," "snack that can be eaten without a fork," and so on, graduating slowly to the final parties' relatively complex spreads of flavored drinks (always nonalcoholic) and utensil-requiring desserts. At the conclusion of each day, all the sorority girls would shut the doors and vote on who was to receive the next morning's bids, and the rushees would return home to stress out over it.

It was draining, to say the least. My feet hurt from all the walking up and down Sorority Row. I fretted over spinach between my teeth, dumb comments I'd made, bad hair days, scuffed and/or unfashionable shoes, and the other, cuter, blonder, better-dressed girl who was getting more smiles than I from the active members. In the midst of being overwhelmed by all this, I was pretty clueless as to which house I would end up in, if any—a detachment that allowed me to mentally distance myself from the whole thing. I watched these girls singing sorority-modified versions of the theme from *Ice Castles*, and decided I'd rather be at a Love and Rockets show. The whole shebang was odd, but I figured, that's just how rush is—these girls don't actually live like this day-to-day. With some effort, I could see through the hoo-ha and view them as normal women.

At the end of the seemingly eternal process, my high school buddies had all been sorted into houses. Though a bit more tentatively than they, I, too, decided to go forward and give the whole thing a whirl. I received a bid from a house—let's call it Sorority X (you'd pronounce it "Sorority Chi," of course)—whose members seemed cool and smart enough. Maybe a little conservative, but in retrospect, I'm not sure what else I was expecting. I figured accepting a bid seemed harmless.

But once I picked up my final bid on the last day and sat down at their balloon-bedecked welcome-aboard tea party, I was no longer just another rushee but a potential member of the sisterhood (I was now a pledge—still not a full member yet). It was really overwhelming to first set foot into this ostensibly happy and close-knit family, especially when the sisterhood thing is repeated so often and institutionally, as if saying "sisterhood" a lot will make it real. Sororities take this stuff seriously: If you become an active member at one house, you're not allowed to just drop out and join another one later. This even applies if you switch schools, so you really don't want to screw up. It's weird to witness this abrupt sense of responsibility during rush, and it's really, really weird to be plunged into it on your first day as a pledge.

Surrounding me were more than a hundred young ladies I'd never spent more than ten minutes with—and one of them, who apparently had a leadership role, stood up and told me to look around at my new lifelong friends. Frankly, I didn't see anything wrong with the old ones who were part of my actual, you know, *life,* but those three were all simultaneously listening to similar speeches, in various states of joy and disappointment, at other houses up or down Sorority Row. The four of us, who in high school all had fairly similar GPAs, activities, and, therefore, positioning in the school's social strata, ended up in sororities that were strikingly different from one another. One was a "top house" with wealthy cheerleader types; one—mine—was kind of middle-of-the-road as far as sororities go; and the third, where the two least-close friends pledged, leaned toward brainy. The whole point of rush is to condense the natural selection process by quickly gathering together like-minded women, so it seemed odd how we'd each ended up with whole houses of girls we wouldn't necessarily have chosen if left to our own devices.

Why is this? Rushers and rushees don't have much to go on in their brief encounters (I experienced this from the other direction the following year, when I was in the position of having to interview pledges). You judge by superficialities, working with what few cues you've got, such as what someone is wearing, what activities she did in high school, and where she's from. As a result, cute, cheerleader-type girls get into houses with other cute, cheerleader-type girls. Geeks end up with geeks. Women from prominent families tend to have really good rushes, even when they're not really that pleasant to be around. Partly this all is due to the old-school mentality of the 40- and 50-something ex-sorority women who come back to supervise the rush process and make sure the "right" women get in, but it's also the speed involved. Though my friends and I had known and loved one another since third grade as well-rounded, complex people, our external traits apparently connoted wildly different things to the RLU sorority establishment. As with a singles' bar or speed-dating event, the compatibility success rate is not going to be as high when you go this route as when people actually spend time together and bond.

Ostensibly, though, bonding is what the several-weeks-long pledge period is for. This lasts for about a semester, and it's a limbo time during which pledges go to activities at the house and get to know the active members before having yet become full members themselves. Theoretically, there can still be a parting of the ways during this period, but it doesn't happen too frequently. Most pledge classes have one or two de-pledges, usually for financial or time-commitment reasons, and although the house can still kick you out, it's only done when a girl infringes in a big way—murder, drug possession, that sort of thing. Being unmasked as a member of another sorority at the school you transferred from will get you booted, too. Just being a bitch or a pain in the ass (which pledges are, frequently) isn't enough to get you tossed, so a girl who looked great on paper might really end up a thorn in the other ladies' sides. For life.

During the pledge period, we did lots of organized activities specially designed to facilitate sister-bonding: mini-seminars on the house history, special pledge-only dinners, parties for the whole house. We took a couple of weekend trips off campus. We went through whatever hazing was allowed within the Panhellenic Council's carefully specified antihazing rules, which are so military as to make the snack thing look slipshod. Members were allowed to make us wear the house colors every day, carry candy to hand out to members who asked, answer the phone with our sorority's name, get woken up for little excursions—benign stuff, yet annoying enough that even the most rah-rah pledges tried to weasel out of doing them. Even so, these rituals were much, much kinder than the fraternity hazings we'd hear rumors of, many of which involved varying combinations of fear, discomfort, and/or private parts.

After all these bonding opportunities, most of us found at least one fellow pledge we liked out of a group of 40 or 50, except for those who insisted on being real curmudgeons. (I gave it a good shot, and still found pledges I liked.) Women who go through rush in the first place tend to be socially skilled, and everyone else was seeking out her place too, meaning that most pledges were trying to play nice and make friends.

Which isn't to say that everyone actually accomplished this. Although you'd imagine a sorority to be one gigantic in-crowd, cliques and stratifications happened within each house, forming a neat little microcosm of the university. My house was no exception. There were always a few Muffy Tepperman–esque super-sisters who ran for elected house offices; shy, studious types who were usually really nice; flaky girls who nobody ever saw at the house (mostly burnt-out seniors busy worrying about the real world); girls with, you know, reputations among the frat boys; hippie girls (relatively speaking); nerds (again, relatively speaking); brains; jocks—you name it. There were definitely the cool girls, the not-so-cool girls, and the "legacies"—girls automatically accepted because their mother or sister is a member—always a real crapshoot. And despite all the kum-bah-ya of the various candlelit ceremonies, those groups didn't really mix all that well. Throw a couple of ex-boyfriend frat boys and some bad keg beer into the mix, and it was all shot to hell.

So, knowing this, what makes all the organized rigmarole a beneficial way to set up your social life? In the real, non-Greek world, college students do things like live in the dorms, go to class, work at the student store, study in the library, and join the ski club. They interact with people of both genders, make new best friends, get in fights, laugh, cry, get plastered, make bad decisions, suffer from homesickness, and generally live out the wildly vacillating range of emotions you have in your late teens and early twenties. And they find plenty of kindred spirits to share these experiences with organically, without forced friend-making activities or an officially sanctioned weeding-out process. In fact, it's those without the social skills to do this on their own who'd most benefit from a sorority-type organization to help them out, but they're the ones least likely to get in. In all honesty, it's hard to justify a real need for sororities in this day and age. There are the presumed benefits of networking, whether for jobs, social purposes, or whatever, but again, the university itself provides plenty of opportunities to make appropriate connections for later in life. And sorority girls usually make plenty of friends outside their house as well, so it's not as though you couldn't schmooze with them anyway if that's your main goal. Sororities do "make a big school a little smaller"—but if that's an issue, you might as well be at a smaller school in the first place.

As far as lifelong sisterhood—well, fourteen years later I still am really close with one fellow Sorority Xer, but that doesn't demonstrate much of a batting average for a 150-girl house. Heck, I've got at least one close friend from every job I've held since then, and that wasn't even the goal of the screening process that got me in those doors.

Strangely, though, my fellow sisters do pop up from time to time in my life. I went to a networking event a while back and a woman I didn't recognize turned to me and mouthed silently, "You were in my sorority." She was right; I was. We were even in the same pledge class. Her hair was an entirely different color and style than it had been in college, she was dressed a little groovier and less sororityish than I remember (yeah, external cues, I know), and we had gone into the same industry. Truth be told, I hadn't been all that wild about her during our sorority years, finding her a bit standoffish and more in with the cool kids than I was, but now that we've grown up and expanded into the greater world a bit, I actually like her a lot. We even hang out socially.

So what does that say about creating your own sisterhood? Probably not much—or maybe just that it isn't really one continuous lifelong bond but lots of little interactions that pop up over the course of your time on the planet. Or maybe it's just a sales pitch. Who knows? During your life, it's a given that people will come and people will go, including sisters—both real and fake.

Le Divorce

Karen Eng

On a chilly September evening in 2000, on the last day of my honeymoon, I hiked alone up and down the small, hilly streets of Halifax, Nova Scotia. My head pounded as I walked, and I saw nothing but my feet hitting the sidewalk.

When my new husband and I had first arrived at the Halifax hostel, the first thing I did was check my e-mail, eager to enjoy postwedding debriefings from friends and family. There was a message, as always, from Rizzo, my best friend from college and my most faithful correspondent. Rizzo, who'd traveled halfway around the world from her home in Paris to attend my wedding in California.

I opened her e-mail to read a brief, chatty note describing her holiday adventures after my husband and I had left for Canada—in the midst of which she tossed in a mention that, by the way, she'd spent the night that week with someone I'd been involved with on and off over the past seven years. "In your bed," she took pains to point out, along with details of how far things had progressed sexually. "God, he's vulnerable, isn't he?"

I felt gored, not because I had any residual romantic feelings for the man in question—in fact, it could have been any guy she'd known I'd had a significant past with—but because of this distinctly aggressive act on her part. There was no note of warm co-conspiracy here, no apology that my honeymoon might not be the time to make such an announcement, no hint of concern for my feelings. More than anything, I was furious that she had, despite all my efforts, successfully made herself the center of my attention on what was supposed to be a joyous new beginning for me and my husband. I was disgusted at myself for having given her the key to my apartment against my better judgment—but I also felt relieved.

The thing is, I had been half-expecting something like this to happen. The pressure had been slowly building in this friendship we'd sustained over a dozen years and two continents. It was really only a matter of time before she finally gave me a reason to break it off for good.

From the beginning, I considered Rizzo an extraordinary person. We met when we were both about twenty, transfer students to UCLA, at a time when I was still in a pupal stage between unsure-of-myself Catholic schoolgirl and what I imagined to be confident, worldly womanhood. We'd been hired by the university for a peer-tutoring program and were trained in a group of about ten other undergraduates. Being singled out as clever made us all a little cocky and clubby. For a time we moved in a pack, cracking such jokes as only undergraduate liberal arts majors would consider funny—egging each other on with runaway puns and bad-Hemingway riffs. But being accepted into this friendly, witty circle allowed me to consider myself, however tentatively, one of the smart ones.

So when Rizzo made the extra effort of inviting me out to an art gallery one weekend, it felt like being chosen by the head of the class to be her vice president. In a group of already strong personalities, she was clearly a leader, and temperamentally my opposite in many ways. First of all, the fact that she was studying poli-sci gave her an intellectual air, especially in contrast to my flaky poetry major. Her manner was brash and a little aggressive as she argued with and chummed up to our middle-aged bosses; I was easily cowed by authority. While I was relatively reticent, she spoke her mind loudly, with a don't-care attitude and a caustic sense of humor. I loved how her cackle resounded through the halls.

In my first visits to her place, she introduced me to a world that seemed impossibly together and sophisticated for someone our age. She lived in a converted Spanish-style stucco house in Los Angeles's hip Melrose neighborhood, far from the dorms and student apartments, safe in the shadow of campus. She'd attended high school in Paris, where her parents still lived. She called them by their first names. She offered to make me cups of Lapsang Souchong tea and cooked with Roma tomatoes, neither of which I'd ever heard of. She had her very own beige-box Mac, a serious luxury for a student in those days. She was highly organized and seemed ready to face any eventuality: She kept on hand not only stamps but a postal scale, was savvy about car maintenance, and kept a shoebox full of flavored condoms under her bed, in preparation for the lovers who would surely materialize. I'd never met anyone so fervently in control of life.

Slowly we began spending more time alone than with the gang. It started with her inviting me over to type my papers on her computer. Suddenly, with no transition that I can remember, we seemed to be practically living together. I'd go over with my laundry and homework, and we'd manage to fit grocery shopping, cooking, studying, baths, face masks, and gossip into each overnight. She'd lend me her dad's flannel pajamas and we'd lie together on her double futon (another nod to adulthood; everyone else I knew still slept on a twin mattress), talking late into the night before falling asleep. The next morning she'd make me coffee and drive the forty-five minutes across town to school like a maniac.

Everything that seemed overwhelming about grown-up life—all the mundane activities and errands—now seemed not only doable, but glamorous. On top of that, Rizzo took care of me. If I was hungry, she made me lunch. If I wasn't getting along with my roommates, she'd urge me to stay with her. If I was nervous about a doctor's appointment, she insisted on coming into the exam room with me to hold my hand and argue on my behalf, if need be. If I was upset with my parents or a love interest, she took my side with a ferocity that made my eyes water.

Blinded as I was by my admiration of her and flattered by the intimacy she bestowed on me, I didn't fully understand the extent to which this remarkable self-sufficiency camouflaged a dangerously insecure, self-destructive young woman. But there were signs. She loved brightly colored garments and lipstick, which likened her look to those poisonous creatures whose garishness warns off predators. Sometimes she'd turn her ironic humor on herself with uncomfortable sharpness. Hoping to get her to stop, I'd respond by whapping her hard enough to sting—a sort of reverse Pavlovian experiment. "Ow!" she'd giggle, laughing and rubbing her arm as our friends watched in shock.

She aimed her scathing wit outward as well. A good portion of our private conversations included her disproportionately harsh, mean-spirited comments about our peers, fairly minor things—their immaturity, or bad manners, or pretentious choice of academic pursuit. Upon meeting anyone new, she would size them up, either deeming them amazing and worthy (what happened to me, I suppose) or smirking and finding fault. I can't remember a single person we knew in college who fell somewhere in between, though I remember clearly those who fell from favor. As the force of her ire became more apparent, I became terrified of that happening to me. As intimidating as she could sometimes be, you either stayed out of her way or stayed close, right in the eye of the hurricane. I chose the latter.

What did I have to offer Rizzo? Emotional ballast, I think. For all my unworldliness—or maybe because of it—I did have a boundless sense of optimism that she lacked. This became clear when her crying jags began, usually triggered by episodes in one or another ongoing drama of unrequited love. Her big personality didn't translate—always to my surprise—into lots of interested men, and for those who were intrigued, their liking her pretty much guaranteed her rejecting them. The men she did fall for were always unattainable in some way: either gay, or married, or another friend's love interest. She would write impassioned letters to them, which they always seemed to ignore, triggering deep-seated self-esteem and abandonment anxieties. The intensity of her preoccupation was such that I can still name the objects of her doomed desire in chronological order. It was an exasperating state of affairs. No matter how much time I spent trying to talk her out of her depression and fears, her hopelessness only grew, utterly out of proportion to the crisis at hand, considering there had usually never been a relationship in the first place.

So I shouldn't have been surprised, during one of these episodes of despair, when she began admitting to suicidal thoughts. Phrases like "I don't want to live" began slipping out. She'd been seeing a therapist, but it didn't seem to do any good. She tried antidepressants, but she said they gave her terrible side effects. She never actually attempted suicide, but I remember her state over the year before we graduated as a blur of stubborn hopelessness.

Close friendships between women often rely on some sort of dichotomy in order to work—she was the intellectual urbanite, I was the hapless hippie—and to some extent it's what creates the whorl of excitement and mutual support. But as her depression worsened, the comparisons became more accusatory. Mostly they took the form of: "You wouldn't understand because you've never been alone: You've always had a boyfriend," a statement that would become a mantra right up to the very end. In fact, it wasn't true—but that didn't matter. The seeds of resentment and guilt had been planted.

Yet her possessiveness never manifested itself in her not wanting me to have relationships. The only thing that seemed important to her was that she stay number one, that our bubble was unburstable—the tacit understanding that the men in my life were temporary visitors, and when it came down to it, she would come first. Abandonment was out of the question. This didn't strike me as being particularly unreasonable, given the intensity of our relationship. We were, after all, just laying the foundations for the ultimate, *Thelma and Louise* ideal of friendship between women, promising to be available to each other no matter what—especially when it came to men—even if it meant going over a cliff together. At this point, I was more than willing to trade the sense of protection and excitement she offered for anything she could demand of me above and beyond the bounds of normal friendship, no matter how all-consuming. Anyway, I didn't want normal. I thought Rizzo's taking up a lot of mental and emotional space in my life meant that we had an extra-special friendship, and I placed a high value on that. It made me feel worthy: Someone I looked up to so much needing me elevated me, too.

It also helped that, while we spent a lot of time together, we were never exclusive. Once the foundation of our friendship was established, we gradually spent more and more time apart in different social circles. I became friends and roommates with another fellow tutor, and Rizzo cultivated friendships in a more politically oriented crowd. The space we learned to give each other is probably what helped our relationship thrive after college, when she moved back to Paris. Regardless, I was starting to feel exhausted and oppressed by her constant negativity and threats of self-harm. So when I was offered the chance to move to Northern California, I took it eagerly, in part because I needed to get away from her.

I suppose, if I'd wanted to, that I could have let the relationship drift after graduation. It could have been easy, separated by an ocean. But the distance was apparently just what was needed. We fell into writing each other long letters. These were more like journals, the obsessive recording of the details of our lives. The letters spanned days and sometimes weeks, resulting in invitingly bulging packets that arrived twice a month. Writing turned out to be the natural evolution of our relationship and it suited us perfectly. We had ample room to pursue other friendships while keeping each others' full attention, and the thousands of miles between us gave me room to feel supportive and supported without getting too swept up in her mood swings.

Then e-mail came along, making it possible for us to keep a volley of communication going at all hours, multiple times a day, sometimes allowing flurries of conversation when we both happened to be up across time zones. At a time when people were just starting to navigate the weird soul-to-soul, ethereal intimacy of online relationships, Rizzo and I were achieving a mind-meld. We started using the term "best friend." It was a big deal to me, though it happened without fanfare— one of us just dropped it into conversation, in passing, as in, "I told the people at work my best friend was coming to visit from overseas so I needed some days off." To me, the term connoted not just the first person you'd turn to with good news or a crisis, but in our case, the person who'd be ready to drop everything and take you in at any moment. That's who we'd become for each other.

We'd travel to visit each other every couple of years, and we'd fall right back into sharing a bed—displacing any boyfriend or lover that happened to be around at the time. We'd shop and cook and gossip and joke as usual, punctuated by Rizzo's slides into despondence and occasional outbursts of resentment. I distinctly remember our bedtime conversations: her lying on her back in her pjs, tears running out of the corners of her eyes as she wept silently. Her depression had become inevitable, and even though I always stayed on alert for spikes, I always tried to accommodate it, balancing any tilts by acting, as much as possible, as if everything were normal. For years she'd told me she didn't really plan suicide attempts; she just often found living too much to bear. She insisted she was too much of a coward to carry it out. It was a small comfort, but I clung to it anyway. "I love you and I want you to be happy," I'd say.

Almost a decade went by like this, and the dynamic we had put into motion in our youth remained pretty much intact as we got older. Our correspondence consisted of e-mails throughout the week, phone calls at least twice a month, the occasional handwritten letter, gifts of books, recipes, and an occasional sex toy—whatever we thought would make the other person laugh. It was a more delicate balance than I realized at the time. Amid the fun and the standard girlfriend commiserations, a good portion of time was allocated to her ups and downs—not the regular setbacks of life, or even the big catastrophes, which we both had, but the nameless great depressions, which could as easily be triggered by minor incidents as major ones.

Ironically, all the skills being her friend had taught me—the courage to move through life with chutzpah, the ability to articulate my sense of injustice—allowed me to get a perspective on her dilemma, and that perspective was making me uneasy. We were nearing our thirties, and if anything, things were the same to worse. Her emotional states became more extreme—dynamic and happy one minute, sullen and desperate the next, with the bad moods winning out over the good ones more and more.

I also started noticing that every time I told her of something going on in my life, good or bad, she would compare it against her own likes, dislikes, and value system. Up until then, I had always seen her make genuine efforts to push aside her crises to listen to my problems, though mine always seemed to pale in comparison. But now she couldn't just be empathetic and supportive. Every conversation somehow swung back to being about her, and the old accusation that I always seemed to have what she didn't lurked uncomfortably close to the surface. Was it a way of bringing us into some kind of weird equilibrium?

It got to the point where I felt I couldn't tell her anything. Eventually I stopped reporting my every problem and triumph to Rizzo, even failing to share the news that I had met the man I would ultimately marry. She seemed in such a bad state, I just chickened out of telling her. I had started to see that only setbacks won me points, while my happiness made me the target of barbed remarks or fed into her bad moods. I wanted to enjoy my new relationship for as long as I could without letting this intrude.

So when she flew over for my thirtieth birthday, I braced myself. I would finally have to introduce her to my boyfriend, who was about to move in with me. It was a tricky visit. For the first time, I didn't ask the man in my life to sleep elsewhere so that Rizzo could sleep with me, as was our tradition. It was a silently significant moment—someone had taken her place. It wasn't easy for him, either. He'd had my full attention for months, and here was this intimidating, intense woman vibrating in our bower. Instinctively, he stayed out of the way.

But the birthday party was a big success: To my friends she showed her sparkling personality. She cut an impressive figure—stylish, cultured, hilariously witty, charming, attentive, ultra-modern, and independent. She was scintillating and wry and hyperintelligent, the Rizzo I'd fallen in love with so long ago. But after the guests left and she was alone with me, she became contemptuous, sullen, rancorous. Something shifted. I was starting to understand how brittle her colorful surface was. I started to sense that maybe she didn't like me anymore. The sense of safety was falling away: For the first time, I saw clearly how I bore the brunt of her darkness while the rest of the world got to enjoy her bright side. I had no frame of reference for how to deal with it. And I was starting to resent it.

Some will say I should have broken it off with her then. But it wasn't as easy as that. First of all, I couldn't have articulated my darkening feelings so clearly at the time. Second, we were emotionally intertwined, and there were so many circumstances that kept us in a lock: our long history, my having held her on a pedestal, and having felt as though I owed my confidence to her. Besides, the moment someone is threatening to commit suicide is not the moment to dump her or even confront her. With Rizzo that moment was always imminent, so it never seemed like an option.

In fact, a few months after she returned to Paris she hinted that she was making actual plans to kill herself at last. Though her calls were difficult and despairing, I kept her on the phone for as long as I could, irrationally hoping I would be postponing the worst as the seconds ticked by. Most terrifyingly, she sent me a duplicate of a letter she'd sent to her lawyer, changing her will to include me. I had to face the possibility that her suicide might actually happen. I was frozen with fear and guilt—and growing rage that she was still putting me through this.

I also worried that all this agonizing was taxing my other friendships and my new relationship. Hoping for emotional support and guidance, I began consulting a therapist, who helped me see that my friend very likely had a clinical condition. She may not be conscious of it, she told me, but she wants your attention. She needs to be at the center. "If you give her a hand, she'll eat your arm," were her exact words. That's a condition of being her friend right now, she said—if it becomes too destructive to your life, however, you can walk away. This didn't make sense to me. As she said, depression is an illness. If Rizzo had another disease that made her extra-needy, and being with her less than pleasant, would I walk away from that? What kind of person—what kind of friend—would I be?

Instead of walking away, I invited her to come back to California. I took her to a hot spring resort outside of town for a few days, thinking a little nature might do her good, and we could enjoy some quality time alone. But almost as soon as we were by ourselves, she became her old, mean, self-pitying self—hardly the fragile creature I thought I was trying to talk back from the ledge. We went home in near silence. Upon arrival, we were met with terrible news: A friend of mine had died suddenly. As I tried to sort out my feelings, Rizzo yammered about coming with me to the wake for a man she'd only known of through my involvement with his family, about whom she'd never had anything nice to say. I'm sure that, in her mind, she wanted to be there to support me—a reflex from the old days. To my mind, she could feel me turning my attention away and desperately needed to be number one, to be in my radar, to have my attention. It was too much. My friend was actually dead, while Rizzo was very much alive and had just put me through this useless trip. I had to say *no* repeatedly before she understood and backed off. At that moment, I didn't care what she did. *Go ahead and kill yourself,* I thought. *I'm done.*

So for the first time in our friendship, I asked for some space, and to my stunned surprise, she acquiesced. Maybe the make-nice, accommodating spirit of girlish friendships worked, after all, and all I'd had to do was ask. For the better part of a year, the e-mails trailed off, and our conversations were lighter and less frequent. It was a big relief to have the pressure off, and for the moment, everything seemed to be okay.

But then my boyfriend and I got engaged. Even though I was enjoying life without so much Rizzo in it, I couldn't *not* tell her, or not invite her to the wedding. But given her bizarre behavior, I couldn't help wondering whether she'd try to somehow hijack or disrupt the wedding party. Would she do something wildly inappropriate?

The wedding actually went pretty smoothly. Rizzo was in her best upbeat party mode and everyone had a good time. I berated myself for thinking such awful thoughts and relaxed into my honeymoon. Then I got the e-mail. And when I got home, well, let's just say she certainly didn't need to leave the condom packets scattered around my otherwise fastidiously made bed.

All I wanted to hear, those first few weeks, was any inkling that she might understand how I could feel violated and disturbed. Though I was devastated by the implications, I wanted to give her the benefit of the doubt. I let it stew for a few days, and when the time came, I was as measured as I could muster, explaining to her over the phone that it wasn't the act, but the way it was undertaken—especially the way she told me. She could have waited until after my honeymoon. She could have taken a less cavalier tone. She could have gone to his bed, a mile away. She didn't need to leave the condoms out.

If she had said immediately that any one of these things might have been a weird and insensitive thing to do, there could have been a chance. Instead, she argued me down vehemently, her main defense being that there was no possible way she could have had any idea that this would upset me so much—thereby nullifying thirteen years of supposed intimacy. After this, she suddenly became pally and jokey, acting as though we were as tight as ever, and, leaning toward my old trust in her, I almost bought it. But by the time I hung up, I knew that instead of calming my suspicions, the conversation had confirmed them.

The problem with the *Thelma and Louise* metaphor is that, no matter how glamorous Susan Sarandon and Geena Davis look doing it, they ultimately go off a cliff. For those of us living in the real world, it's not really a good ending. Rizzo was scary and irrational, and it was never going to end. I wanted out of the car. But how?

The therapist had suggested that if I had really made up my mind to break it off, I should just drift—"become boring," in her words—the classic polite-but-chilly treatment we learn as girls and take into womanhood. But that just felt like it would lead to more years of lying and walking on eggshells, which I already felt deeply ashamed of and needed to put a stop to, pronto. Besides, if I felt justified enough to walk away from a thirteen-year friendship, I felt obliged to say why. I owed her that much, in spite of everything, and I would have expected the same.

What not even the therapist understood was that I needed a divorce. There is no other word that better expresses the magnitude of what was happening. By her presence in my life, Rizzo had made me feel at home in the world. In return, I'd hoped to do the same, and had been determined to be faithful to her for better or for worse. Cutting her out of my life would be tantamount to cutting a chunk of myself away. We had lived far too much of our emotional lives together to end it by just "forgetting" to call. This needed to be a permanent, final, life-changing break—the kind you get from an abusive husband—requiring paperwork and planning. But women friends don't get divorced. If we had that option, maybe I wouldn't still be in this mess.

In any case, nobody could tell me how. The phone was no good: This had to be well thought-out, and besides, I was too susceptible to her charm, and too scared of her anger. It would have to be a letter, and because I wanted her to get it as soon as possible, it would have to be e-mail. In the weeks that followed, I hashed it over with my therapist, with my friends, with my husband, with my sister. I wrote draft after draft, e-mailed it around for edits. I wanted to say, finally, exactly how taken advantage of and disrespected I felt. I asked her not to contact me. And then I clicked Send. I stopped answering the phone, destroyed or sent back letters unopened, programmed my e-mail to bounce her messages back, and told our few mutual friends that I wanted no information to pass back and forth between her and me. At the same time, I was petrified that this would be the thing that would finally, ironically, send her over the edge. But it was worth facing that fear if it meant I could get control.

Six months later, of course, she called. I couldn't hang up, as hard as I tried to force myself to. I could hear myself breathing down the receiver. She wanted to know whether we could be friends. I said no.

"Why not?"

"Because I can't say no to you. Because I can't even hang up the phone."

"Not now, or never?"

The therapist had told me to expect this question. I took a deep breath and said what she'd drilled me to say—"Not now, and maybe never."

Maybe, I said, years down the line—if our lives are really different, and things have drastically changed. But for now, we're just not good for each other. I did manage to tell her one more time that I loved her and wanted her to be happy. I even remember us laughing, and how good it felt. She said she hadn't been suicidal in a long time, and it had been because of me. She said she knew she had put too much on me at times, and she was sorry for that. She said she had a boyfriend, and that she was happy. I told her I was truly happy for her, and I was, in the way that a part of us never stops caring for our exes. Then I hung up the phone.

Unplanned Unparenthood

Jennifer D. Munro

O n my due date, I go to the circus. Not the three-ring circus of my youth with geriatric lions and lame clowns, but a slick, traveling Las Vegas circus. Everything's in French, which makes the show somehow classier, elevating both its panache and its ticket price. At Bahama Breeze, a joint with vertical food, tricolored drinks, and enthusiastic waiters in puka shell chokers, we shoot the shit before the show. I've been looking forward to this evening for a long time—just the six of us girls, ogling the codpieces and bitching about how men never change the vacuum-cleaner bags.

I haven't met one of the women before. She orders water, then announces that she's pregnant. Amid squeals of excitement from the other women—who are mothers, or speak of their future motherhood with certainty, as I used to—my heart sinks, although I don my good-sport mask, smiling and murmuring my congratulations.

It's my due date, but I'm not pregnant anymore. This last miscarriage was my seventh in ten years. It was the most physically taxing, too: I'm still struggling with anemia as a result of the blood I lost along with the baby. It's finally become obvious to me that I'll never be a mother, although I suppose this might have occurred to someone less obtuse and optimistic quite some time ago. With this last loss, some impatient but merciful god finally threw a hammer at my head, thundering, "Enough already! Get on with your life!" I blinked, shook my head, and said, "Well, duh." When you're caught in the riptide of pregnancy attempts and infertility treatments, it's easy to lose perspective.

I haven't figured out exactly what getting on with my life means just yet, except for diligent contraception. I have sad moments, but I don't pass my days in dirgeful mourning, or dwell on wishful thinking for what can't be. But today of all days, when I wanted to get out and distract myself with a blue drink and buff men in leotards, it's hard to feel celebratory about someone else's pregnancy.

I deal with childlessness pretty well most other days. After all, I'm not Anne Boleyn about to lose my head because I can't produce a prince. In the United States in the twenty-first century, my life is not without value simply because my uterus has a mind of her own. She has demonstrated repeatedly that she is adamantly, stridently opposed to motherhood. She wants a motorcycle. She wants to be a badass poet living life on the fringe in Amsterdam. She wants a lesbian affair. She wants her own damn room. She threw tantrums and pitched out the babies along with the bathwater. So be it.

Still, the fact that I'll never bear a child does make me a misfit among my friends. Having met as young women who drank and gossiped throughout our twenties, artists and writers who dreamt of creative success, we clicked immediately upon introduction because we saw that telltale, bohemian, "wanting something different" look in each other's eyes. Then our biological clocks went off with screaming persistence, and it turned out we wanted the same thing as every other woman, after all.

We thought we were turning on our blinkers at about the same time and taking the same turnoff toward motherhood. I missed the exit by biological accident. I bumbled along in the dark with my motherhood blinker going, going, going for years, driving myself and everyone behind me crazy with my false signal, which I couldn't switch off. We all thought I was going to turn, but I didn't. In the meantime, all my married women friends have either had kids or are anxiously awaiting pregnancy when the time is right, their refrigerators plastered with photos of babies produced by friends and relatives like an extension of their magnetic to-do list. There were bound to be some collisions as a result—and there's only so much impact friendships can withstand.

With several of my close friends, children certainly would have sealed our bond. One friend and I conceived within days of each other. Though I had already miscarried once, I was certain that my second pregnancy would have no problems; I'd had several friends who had miscarried and then gone on to have a baby. We were both thrilled about the timing. These babies would cement our friendship for life—they would practically be twins, growing up together. We'd share profound experiences and challenges—pregnancy, birth, and all that motherhood entails.

Her son is now eight years old, and I haven't seen her in years. We used to walk the lake together frequently before she got pregnant, but then she and her husband began walking weekly with another set of expectant parents. I passed them once, strolling the other way. Soon-to-be-dads walked up front, while the expectant moms waddled along behind. We made polite but awkward small talk, then said goodbye. Our paths, and our lives, continued in opposite directions. We floundered through a few attempts to maintain the friendship, but we simply drifted apart. The last time I saw her—a rare date when she escaped the house to meet me for a margarita—she confessed that her ideal get-together with a girlfriend was having the friend pick her up and drive her to Costco, where they could gab while they pushed their shopping carts up the aisle together. She flat-out admitted that was all she could handle for the time being. I admired her candor, her ability to recognize her limits and stick to them rather than trying to run herself even more ragged out of guilt, as so many women do.

I also felt guilty. If I'd been a good person, a self-sacrificing friend, I would have eased her load and taken her to Costco on a regular basis. But I hate Costco. I'd rather pay an inflated price and walk to the corner market. I hate driving, and at the time, I rarely had access to a car. I would have been miserable trying to meet her needs and dispense with mine. I can be selfless; I can and do go out on limbs for friendships, but I didn't feel that my childlessness and her motherhood should suddenly relegate me to the rank of childless aunt. I had not played that role in our relationship before the baby, and it wasn't a role I ever wanted to play—although I find that I'm frequently expected to play it now.

I might have made different choices had I known I was traveling toward a dead end. I could have put more energy into becoming the favorite auntie to everyone else's kids, for example. I could have been primary babysitter, godmother, emotional rock for my friends' mothering woes. I could have remembered birthdays, spoiled the toddlers. But I didn't. There were logistical complications: my lack of a car, their living across town, and so forth. Maybe if I hadn't been so busy with my own decade-long crisis—painful tests, therapies that did no good, and physical and emotional recoveries that took time and solitude—I could have been available and selfless. On the other hand, maybe if my friends hadn't already become mothers, they could have been available and selfless for me, too.

All but the pregnant woman at Bahama Breeze know about my recent miscarriage, but no one mentions it. It hangs over our plantain spears like an open parenthesis that's never filled in or closed—the awareness is there, but it is left unspoken. They spend the rest of dinner talking about morning sickness and babysitters. Having nothing to contribute, I'm silent. With my newfound acceptance that I'll never be a mother, I have no idea where I fit in anymore. All conversation leads to babies.

At one point, my friend mentions that I'm a writer. She's probably trying to be kind by bringing the conversation around to a subject I can partake in. The expectant mom asks what I write about. Telling her that I write about my seven miscarriages seems cruel: It's her day, and she has enough to worry about without my sledgehammer of dark possibilities. While I don't want infertility to define me, I do want my experiences to be acknowledged as part of who I am. Still, blurting out that I should be giving birth today instead of belting down slushy Bahama Mamas would be a sure conversation stopper. I could more easily bring up cock rings or farts.

As I struggle with myself over all this, I feel a flicker of annoyance. Her good news has dampened my night on the town because it reminds me of what I wanted to forget. But I don't want to dampen her night, or everyone else's. *This* is how I'm a good friend. So instead of telling her about my miscarriage essays, I tell her that I publish erotic stories—which is also true—and suddenly the table of maternal women is all ears. I am unique in their experience, with my literary smut on sale at the local Barnes & Noble. I am different. I don't fit in. But now I don't fit in because I'm exotic to them, not because I'm tragic. I become the center of attention. My uterus seems well on her way to getting what she wants. Still, what I have seems empty compared to what they have to go home to.

On our way to the circus after the Bahama Breeze, the mothers travel in one car, while the yearning-to-be-mothers ride in another. It's a coincidence based on other factors that the evening's carpool shook out this way. Or perhaps not. Mothers naturally gravitate to each other. I don't really belong in either car, although I have the most fun these days with future mothers. We all want kids but are still free to drink, swear, and stay out late without hassling with child care. I wouldn't really fit into a childless-by-choice car, either. While these make great friends, they say they can't really understand what I'm going through. Besides, they are all very busy writing novels, managing careers, remodeling their houses, maintaining their marriages, and obsessing over their pets. I could hang out with infertile women I've met, but what do we really have to say to each other—other than "Bummer"?

So do I want my friends to bite their tongues around me, as I so often bite mine? I'll be honest: I can be impatient with the thoughtlessness of some friends who have become moms. Mothers justifiably need ears to bend, but it's hard for me to provide the ear. My Costco friend griped often about how much she hated being pregnant. I'd struggle to respond with a reassuring comment, but I could feel my mask cracking.

Another friend spent months on total bed rest with a tenuous pregnancy. The baby would be induced or delivered by Caesarean section as soon as her lungs developed. My friend complained bitterly about the possibility of a C-section. She felt cheated; she had been denied a normal pregnancy, and now she might be denied the experience of a vaginal birth, that seminal rite of passage so many women share, with all its pain and joy. But from my perspective, my friend had everything. The means to carry and deliver the baby, who had miraculously survived, seemed unimportant.

This friend knew my history, although to be fair, we both thought at the time that I'd someday be a mom. She'd even had miscarriages herself. I can't blame her for feeling rather self-involved in the moment, but I was taken aback. Perhaps she thought we were still in the same camp, and that I would appreciate her anxiety better than anybody. I did try, but I couldn't fully comprehend her loss—just as she can now never fully comprehend mine. Her baby finally came by Caesarean, but she has a child, and I have a cat. If she'd chosen to confide her woes to a mutual friend of ours who'd had a joyous home water birth, she would have found a much more supportive shoulder.

* * *

Watching the circus later on, I'm more curious about the female acrobats than the oversized codpieces that must, please god, be stuffed with more than nature's endowments. I wonder if these gaunt women menstruate. What do they do? Surely you can't trust a tampon, flying around on a swing in an outfit like that. Am I unnatural, having thoughts like this? Is there a reason my corrupt genes should not be passed on? I'm fairly certain that the five women I'm with tonight aren't having these thoughts. They're probably thinking about the babies inside them, or those waiting at home.

But I do know this: I could, and would, voice this thought to my gay male friends. I love going out with them because I know the conversation will not inevitably disintegrate into diaper talk. We chat as easily about miscarriages as about cock size. We gab about literature, movies, Enrique Iglesias's mole, and the great guacamole from Costco (which *they* purchase). In fact, our chatter sounds a lot like that of my girlfriends and me before babies came along. We make unforgivable comments about coworkers, moan about cellulite, and swap new drink recipes. They educate me, teaching me about handkerchief color and the meaning of "teabagging." I'm not a tragic figure to them, maybe because they, too, have had to come to grips with childlessness, but they still love their lives.

I've been told that I'm not fat or fashionable enough to qualify as a card-carrying fag hag (there's a compliment in there somewhere), but these days I gravitate more and more to friendships with men, both gay and heterosexual. I don't eschew female friendships—I have many I treasure—but hanging out with the guys is like taking a break, a gulp of fresh air in a smoky, estrogen-clogged room. Our conversation never includes narratives about horrible pregnancies and how that affects having a second child. I can't really participate in recaps of the game, either, but I don't feel bad about missing out on sports. Basketball's not an emotional trigger. Small talk stays on neutral territory, and that's a relief I need for now.

I do believe that friendships are fragile and require mutual nourishment. But how can I feel empathy for something I envy my friends for having? How can I blame them for turning to those who can share their experiences? My friends change roles overnight when they become mothers, and they need women who can support them with their new and demanding responsibilities. There's no halfway with motherhood, it seems, no compromise with a past way of life. Motherhood is a runaway train on a downgrade. I can attempt to lob a loaf of bread through an open window at times, but mostly I'm puttering around on my own ill-laid track, trying to figure out where the hell I'm going.

In the meantime, I do find myself hanging out with quite a few moms who are at the point in their lives where they are trying to define themselves beyond motherhood, so I fit into the wedge where they attempt to exclude their children and become themselves. We leave each other room to figure out who we are becoming now, and we keep each other company.

One of the first questions new women acquaintances ask me is if I have kids. I hate starting out a conversation with what I'm not, with a negative. It's not a question I ask, and it's not a question men tend to ask, even those who are fathers. It makes sense that women are more apt to define themselves by what emerges from their own bodies. Still, what am I? I'm not a mother. Nor am I an aunt figure, or godmother. What I am is a good friend—honest and considerate—as much as I can be, while still being myself.

Ellen & Me

by Ariel Bordeaux

Where the Boys Are

L. A. Miller

Because I'm the baby and the only girl, my brothers are convinced I was a bit of a sissy as a youngster—entering as evidence such facts as my objection to being dangled by my ankles over the stairwell, and my declining participation in sword fights and firecracker wars. (One of the latter left my middle brother hearing-impaired in his left ear.) But by anyone else's standards, I was just as much Huck Finn as I was Harriet the Spy, both of whom I admired. And, correspondingly, as a girl I was just as likely to play sorcery and magic with Edwin through the backyards of our neighborhood, or tromp through the orchard with Andy, as I was to stay up all night applying fake nail tips with Julie or enact dramatic Breyer-horse plots with Lisa. The fact is, and I'm about to make an essentialist argument here, boys and girls offer different things when it comes to friendship, and I relished separately what each group brought to the table: basketball, frogs, homemade explosives, and light arson on the one hand; and bronzing powder, *Charlie's Angels* reenactments, late-night pizza, and Sweet Valley High on the other.

But perhaps more important to me than the activities each gender was partial to were the different mindsets that characterized friendships with girls and boys. Girlhood relationships rely on conspiracy and loyalty, complicated and elaborate story lines that stand in for real life, and the careful politics both best friends and mix-and-match groupings require. There was a fantastic intensity to the devotion girls demanded of me—an intimate, searing kind of relationship forged in sleepovers and whispered dreams. Boys offered a what-you-see-is-what-you-get simplicity that didn't require the same energy—they saw a potent satisfaction in sticks and rocks and dirt, instead of in a more complex imaginary world. As a girl, I carefully balanced the two types, creating a dream palette of well-rounded friendships.

Thankfully, while in high school and college, even in graduate school, I counted many boys in my friendship group. As much as I depended on my girlfriends—my closest friends, after all, were girls—there were always boys there too, providing ballast with their endearing, stoic, physical selves. My girlfriends continued to be the ones I discussed sex with most frankly; when I yelled and sobbed about romantic woes, they were quick and sure with their "I know just how you feel!" support. There were a couple of "best" friends who claimed, and do still, my undying devotion.

But many of my girlfriends still required effort of some sort, and their support always came at a price. The loyalty and dedication that made them such brilliant confidants, it seemed, also made them a bit of work. So, when I needed to escape processing and apologies, I went back to boys. They were comfortable in their bodies in an intoxicating way, given to both adventure and idleness in fits and starts. They often didn't need to "share" feelings, preferring to swallow them and drink problems away. They were all intelligent and funny, all a little bit feminine, though not every one of them would have claimed it.

Some were more attractive than others, but that wasn't what interested me—boyfriends of the romantic sort are not uncomplicated in the least. These were just boys—boys like my brothers, who taught me to shoot and to drink and to swing a bat, who concurred on the merits of fried bologna sandwiches, and who carried my pack on family hikes when the way got too steep or too hard. Matt and David provided Republican fire to fuel my liberal politics. Carlson and Troy shared my love of cycling and my taste for cheap beer. Tate (who would now be termed a metrosexual, I suspect) told excellent jokes and admired my new clothes. Josh was my beard of sorts, squiring me about town when my husband lived two states away. Just boys.

Then, a year after getting married, I moved back to my home state. At twenty-seven, I found myself creating a new friendship group from scratch. It wasn't so bad—I quickly found like-minded women at work, and started rekindling friendships I'd left behind in the city when I'd moved away years before. Yet soon I noticed something missing from my martini-filled evenings, and it was then that I realized that the boys I'd relied on so much in the past were nowhere to be found. Somewhere along the way, the boys had become men, and men, it seems, are deemed inappropriate friendship fodder for a married woman. The only heterosexual men in my life, other than my husband and brothers, came attached as half of a couple. I quickly got the sense that even those men who arrive in this form are not available for individual friendships outside the foursome paradigm. This, it was made somewhat clear to me, is at best weird, and at worst adulterous.

I was devastated when confronted with this dilemma. I didn't consider it an idle threat to my relationship freedom, it's just that I needed male friends in order to maintain some equilibrium in the give-and-take that friends demand. Removing male energy from the equation meant that I was limited in my ability to offset more high-maintenance friends—the incessant talkers and those in perennial crisis, the ones forever on a diet, the ones who melted if I didn't call them often enough, or the ones who regularly rehashed events from ten years ago to prove my inconstancy—many of whom had somehow survived my move and phoned with alarming frequency. And most of whom were women. In my experience, boys don't care if you haven't called in a while, and they're always game to go out. Boys would always prefer to be left out of decisions about what does or does not look good. They often do not ask how your children are doing, but they also do not take offense easily. Boys like going to baseball games, playing poker, and eating fried food.

I can tell your ears are getting all steamy; I can hear it now: *I like playing poker! I love fried food!* Of course you do—and some metrosexuals really care about clothes and children. As I was discovering, the same John Gray binaries that had once delineated my carefully calibrated friendship life also formed the underlying idea behind heterosexual men becoming "dangerous" friends for grown women. This was the theme of the film *When Harry Met Sally*, spoken first by Harry to a winsome and naive Sally: "Men and women can't be friends; sex always gets in the way." When the line is delivered in the movie, viewers are meant to protest, to decry Harry's sexist behavior and mindset. But at some point in our twenties and thirties, otherwise intelligent adults adopt this rationale—the result being that the loose, amorphous stream of friends that at one time serviced all facets of the modern woman is stopped up like a clogged artery. Once the flow ceases, the only way to get the pipeline flowing again is to succumb to the most captive and limited of routes for insuring men are in the picture: couples friends.

This ideology throws us clear back to the fifties—the menfolk huddled around a smoking grill talking about work, while the womenfolk toss salads in the kitchen, tend to the babies, and emote. There is no room in this model for permutation. And as freethinking as my crowd might be, when a new heterosexual couple is introduced into the group, it is still assumed that I will become friends with the woman, and my husband with the man, no matter that the new guy and I are both itching to sneak downstairs and check out the score of the Mariners game, or that Matt and the lady both love Greek poetry and power tools. The dominance of the girlfriends paradigm—that all women love talking on the phone and processing—and the corollary of the Game Boy paradigm—which dictates that all men secretly wish to play video games in their underwear and look at porn—has not waned in the time since Harry made his sexist declaration in the late '80s, a declaration that is, of course, borne in the film by the uniting of the friends as lovebirds in the end. Sure, they drive each other crazy, but the existence of common traits in opposing genders equals love, not friendship. Just as sharing a common gender is supposed to equal a lifelong bond.

As it turns out, there are many women friends who have fallen by the wayside since my marriage and especially since the birth of my son. They are victims to distance and my lack of time for phone calls and e-mailing and spontaneous nights out. One, in particular, greeted news of my pregnancy with the concern that I wouldn't have enough time left for her. Not unsurprisingly, I don't. Many of my old friends who have survived the utter neglect have been, for many aforementioned reasons, men. While my ability to create satisfying cross-gender relationships is hampered greatly by the couples-friends logic, I've been lucky enough to hold on to a few male friends I've known for ten years or longer. While they don't live in the same city or state, occasional visits and e-mails do more than nicely for now. They seem, in fact, to thrive on my inattention, and if months go by without contact, we each know it means nothing more than that we have a lot going on.

Now, I understand that for me to present all men as solid and nondramatic and all women as siphoning off life force like succubi is way over the top, and, as a rule, false. But I do think women are often socialized to subsume themselves to bad relationships, including believing that gender in and of itself is enough to bind two individuals together (or keep them apart). But it could be that there is hope out there on the horizon—if not in the form of men available for friendship, then in the form of women who embody those characteristics I so cherish in the opposite gender. Because the truth is, it's finally dawning on me that the best friendships I've enjoyed in my life can represent the rule, not the exception, regardless of gender.

Going back to my childhood, I have to admit that growing up with brothers made sisterly relationships a bit alien to me. Friends with sisters or who were close with their mothers as girls told me horror stories of jealousy and constant fighting, loyalty battles, and exclusivity. As a result, I eventually came to believe women just behaved differently with one another—more intensely, more emotionally. The bad traits, it seemed, naturally accompanied the best of what women brought to the table: nurturing validation, honest challenges to destructive behavior, intimacy so intense it borders on passion. Popular culture did nothing but reinforce my idea of what women's relationships must be like, from *Three's Company* on up to the Ya-Yas. And I bought it, putting up with far more obsessive neediness, marathon processing, and guilt over the years than is reasonable to expect from anyone. I continually put my own needs to the side. This was certainly not true of all my women friends, but it takes very few rotten apples. (No wonder I relied on those relationships with male friends; they might not have offered a shoulder to cry on, but at least I didn't constantly have to offer my own.) It may have taken me until my thirties to figure this out, it may even have taken the relative absence of male friends in my life, but I now realize that relationships with women don't have to be so demanding and intense: It's been a revelation.

As an example, let me recount the story of a good friend of mine; let's call her Trix. Trix was approached by a newer friend of hers who half-jokingly asked to be her "best friend." Trix responded in kind, outlining some of the "terms" that might seal the deal. What began as a joke became serious, and they set up a phone date—an interview, really—and got down to it. A lawyer and a busy mom, they essentially hashed out a contract. Their relationship was nonexclusive, they agreed, with no minimum phone requirement per week. Quick queries could be e-mailed or phoned in with the expectation that only a direct answer was required—no chitchat or small talk. They discussed important issues and where they came down on each one—seeking similarity but not needing agreement. In the end, they forged an emotional document in the manner of speed-dating, but for their trouble, I must admit, I think they're going to get something that will last a long time. Why? Because they avoided patent-leather expectations about what women want out of relationships with other women, and communicated directly about one another's baseline needs. Now, men would never hash it out in this way—they would never need to. But because of these women's directness, I wager they're never going to spend time with heavy silence on the phone, or replay messages, or reread e-mails trying to suss out hidden meanings—the type of drama that gives women's friendships a bad name.

So I'm reveling in my women friends, both old and new, now that I know drama doesn't have to be the norm. I'm having fun seeing friends who live scattered around the country, and picking up right where we left off six months before. (Sure, we wish we could see each other more often, but we're open to the curves adult life throws us.) I don't mind turning down invitations when I'm too busy or just want to stay home and having my friend say, "I love being told no! " We take turns absorbing one another's ups and downs. I marvel at the directness and clarity of intriguing, dynamic women who cry "Bullshit!" about the pop-culture read on what women want and need, and who state their needs plainly. And while I continue to savor those rare moments out pruning roses with a male friend, while his wife and my husband take the kids to the zoo, I'm using gender less and less as an indicator for what a relationship might hold in store.

Anyone up for a baseball game?

How to Ex Communicate

Sophie Radice

I have never been that keen on my husband's ex-girlfriends. I wouldn't go quite as far as the woman who demanded that her wealthy boyfriend, Edmund Ko, kill his ex-girlfriend in order to prove the strength of his love for her (Ko is now five years into a life sentence for the crime, so that's probably just as well), but I have to admit that I don't particularly enjoy the chance meetings with his past loves at social gatherings or in the park. These women smile and are usually very pleasant, but I feel they have an odd, irritating advantage over my ongoing relationship.

Ex-girlfriends are shrouded in the rose-tinted mist of nostalgia. It inspires a kind of unwavering loyalty in my husband with which I, with all my associations with the grinding domesticity and hurly-burly of normal marital life, simply can't compete.

Of course, for most of us, the very existence of an ex-lover reminds you that there was a time, a mysterious and disconcerting time, when you were not the most important person in your partner's life. With this paranoid, slightly loopy attitude towards exes prevailing, you can imagine that when I learned, almost ten years ago now, that an important extended-family gathering required the presence of one of my husband's first-ever girlfriends, I was less than thrilled. I had heard a lot about this one. She seemed to be at the center of a whole bunch of artistic West Country types who threw pots, wrote poetry, grew their own vegetables, and had the reputation of not suffering fools gladly. I braced myself.

I first glimpsed Maggie across my mother-in-law's lawn, and I could see that we had something in common straightaway—something beyond my husband. It was this: We were both pregnant. She was heavily pregnant, while I was in that awful, sickly, three-month stage. She took one look at me and seemed to know instinctively that if I didn't eat something very soon, I was going to throw up. She quickly produced three cookies and two apples from her bag.

And amazingly, we got on. She was conspiratorial and no-nonsense, as they said, but everything about her disarmed me. We spent the entire evening together. We made each other laugh.

Still, when Maggie invited my husband and me to stay later in the year, I had my reservations. How healthy was it to invite your ex-lover's lover into your life, so wholesale? A not-over-eager five months later I found myself (by then, heavily pregnant) in the car with my son and husband driving down to Dorset to stay with Maggie and her family.

Yet that first weekend—by which time she had a new baby boy on her hands, and I was walking like John Wayne—was a huge success, against all the odds. Maggie and I kind of fell in love. Our stream-of-consciousness chatting patterns complemented each other. Almost from the first, we would follow each other to the loo and stand outside waiting for the other, so that the conversation wouldn't be interrupted, a habit that has endured throughout our nine-year friendship.

There was more to this than the realization that an ex-girlfriend might have some very interesting insights about the person I am constantly trying to understand, or that she could help me claim the time that I didn't know him or his family. Nor was our connection fueled by the idea that it was probably much smarter to be gracious and grown-up about ex-girlfriends; after all, Jerry Hall managed to be kind to all of Mick's exes—even Luciana Morad, the Brazilian model who had his baby.

No, as Maggie says, what really bound us in this unusual relationship was "a superiority complex and an unfashionable morality" (we hate people who sneak around having affairs, or are still snorting coke when they have kids), a burning but as yet unfocused ambition, and the desire not to farm the children out to other people. "God, we sound awful, don't we?" she said.

It started to become a regular thing, this staying with Maggie, her two children, and her husband. He has a reputation for being clever and moody. (At first he would greet me with remarks such as "So when are you leaving?"—but we got used to each other.) As Maggie says, she "likes dark, handsome, brooding men with big thighs," a description that pretty accurately conjures up both her husband and mine.

At least six times a year, Maggie, the kids, and I would get together for a week. In the summer, we'd sit on the yellow sands of the seaside resort of Bournemouth Beach in the southwest of England, which is close to Maggie's house. Perhaps daringly for approaching forty, we wore bikinis. In the winter we sat on the same beach, but right against the sea wall, in massive parkas, eating cake and drinking hot tea in polystyrene cups from the café. We developed our own culture, our own words, our own frame of reference, our own in-jokes.

Most of the time we play very particular games together, like "Would you rather?"—as in, "Would you rather have your hair cut in a skinhead-girl feather cut, or have to wear one of those nylon, flower-pleated dresses with a very thin belt, worn with ankle socks and white sandals?" Or "Drunk Mummies," in which we pretend to be the posh, plastered mothers perhaps more common to our parents' generation. We laugh a lot, until tears drip down our faces, while the kids look bemused and carry on building their sand tunnel to France.

Our relationship has always baffled people. Women seemed shocked that I could be so intimate with someone who has, after all, been pretty intimate with my husband, and men just look scared, perhaps at the thought of their own current partner joining forces with an ex. I do sometimes feel that my husband must regret ever having introduced us. At times, we are a bit witchy and absorbed in each other, and he and Maggie's husband don't get a break. Twice, our rambling conversations have nearly killed us: once when we swam across a bay, talking for over an hour, swam into a swell, and got smashed against the rocks; another time when we hung back on a walk and the wind lifted us up in the air and crashed us down near the edge of a cliff.

But I am funnier with her than I am with anyone else. I feel her approval all the time, and I think, I hope, that she feels mine, equally. We are both judgmental, tactless, and prone to hysterical laughter, and sometimes I think that this may be why my husband chose us both. More than that, I know that I would have lost out on a great deal if I had let a little thing like Maggie having been loved by my husband get in the way of being her friend.

Out of the Ashes

Shira Kozak

I grew up without real girlfriends, a child of an alcoholic father and a strong-willed mother, part of a hushed household. They died early, in their lives and in mine.

Shy, introspective children of secretive households don't make friends easily, and so much loss made me appreciate having close girlfriends in my teens. I learned early that acquaintances are not enough for me. In my mind, there is something missing in a conversation exclusively centered on home decor, what Judy wore to the ballet, and how they've torn up Fifth Avenue again in the dead of winter.

In the last ten years, I've relinquished the friends I had in high school to the changes of college, marriage, divorce, and travel. I am now an Army wife, and I find it extremely difficult not only to keep in touch with those women I'd like to know better, but to find them to begin with. Army life is a vagabond existence; by the time I get settled in a new city, find a job, and begin the hunt to find friend-caliber women, my husband and I are already preparing for another move.

Typically, by the time we leave a duty station, I have no cherished new addresses or phone numbers in my address book.

This was exactly what I thought would happen when we moved to New York City in 1998.

September 11, 2001, was my son's third birthday. I sat on the edge of my bed, half-dressed. I was dreading the day. "I do not want to go to work today," I told my husband, Roy. Holding my hosiery in a limp hand, I looked up at him. He grimaced. This is one of my typical morning complaints; I hated my commute from Brooklyn to Manhattan. Today was different, though: I honestly did not want to leave home. Hindsight is terrific. I will never again override my instincts for safety and self-preservation. For the time being, however, my whining continued. "It's Chris's birthday. I have too much to do to spend eight hours at the office!" It seemed an excellent excuse.

"Just go in, and I'll help you later. What's the game plan? Chicken nuggets and then cake?"

Now I felt ashamed. Surely I could go to Manhattan, handle risk management for eight hours, and take my three-year-old out for chicken nuggets after work. I headed out feeling resigned, to the Two Rector Street building where our Bear Stearns offices were located. The train was slow. Shit. Late again.

No sooner had my butt landed on my seat at work on the twenty-fourth floor of my office building when *boom!* I looked out the windows and saw what looked like a chunk of flaming airplane go flying past. At my urging, our morning conference call was abandoned and my colleagues—Jason, Kerry, and Mike—and I headed for the elevator. We leaned on each other, sweating and trembling, wondering what had just happened. The noise and movement had seemed like a gas explosion, but I couldn't imagine that underground gas explosions involved airline logos.

"What the hell was that?" Jason asked, shaking.

"I don't know, Jas. I think an airplane hit a building!" I answered. The elevator took its time to descend all twenty-four floors, though we futilely pressed the Close Door button every time it stopped. On most of the floors there was no one waiting to get in when the doors opened. When we finally evacuated the building, everyone I had ridden with in the elevator scattered.

I exited onto Rector Street into a different world, one filled with smoke and sirens, and frantic people making frantic phone calls. I called my husband, half-crying but trying not to, telling him my suspicion that this was not an accident. Airplanes do not hit New York City buildings and airplanes do not cross into New York City airspace, possibly the most protected airspace outside of Washington, D.C. This tragedy was a scenario Roy and I had talked about during the years we'd been in the city, that the terrorists who had misfired in the 1993 attack on the World Trade Center would not rest until they got it right. But I had hoped another attack would not come in my lifetime.

I told Roy to turn on the television at work to see if there was any news coverage yet. He said there were no reports, and then he extracted a promise from me to call him back in ten minutes. I agreed, we said I love you, and I put away my phone, not realizing it was on its last power cell. Roy is part of the military intelligence community, and I knew that his office building on Fort Hamilton was a bomb shelter as well as the emergency relocation point for my son's day care facility. If the day care evacuated, my husband and baby would be near one another. With that knowledge, I put my fears for them aside and redirected my mind to figuring out what I needed to do next.

My co-workers milled around the porch of our building bringing news as it trickled in, as bloody, somber-faced people began to arrive in our lower Manhattan district, a little over one block south of the now flaming North Tower. A man collapsed on the tiled portico at my feet, sobbing. I looked at him blankly, in shock myself, and wondered if I should help him. I am trained in first aid, but in the moment I doubted my own abilities—a disjointed response to his injured state.

I looked up. A young woman was standing near the revolving doors I had just come through. She looked scared, uncertain, and very alone. But she also seemed to have a presence of mind the others around us lacked. I made a decision.

"You! Go inside and bring paper towels and water. There's an injured man here," I instructed. The woman returned with the requested items, and together we cleaned up the man, Pat, who had dived under his WTC maintenance truck when the plane hit. He had fallen in the street, so his entire front was covered with blood and bits of glass and metal. He had a large gash in his forehead, the knees of his work trousers were torn and bloody, and he was weeping. I gave him a few sips of a sports drink to help keep him from going further into shock, and held his hand as he described the streets slick with blood, the decapitated bodies. He'd had to step over them to safely make his way down the street.

My telephone rang faintly from the bottom of my purse. My hands were covered in Pat's blood, so I couldn't get to the phone in time. I missed Roy's call—and, it would turn out, the opportunity to talk to him for at least another eight hours. I wanted to ask him what was happening and, more urgently, what I should do. Lord knows I'm not qualified to make these kinds of decisions, I thought. Shouldn't experienced military people point the way?

The chaos moving around me was immense. As a military wife, I had thought I had a grasp on what it was like to be in a war zone, but now I didn't really know where to go or how to respond. A few minutes later, an EMT looking for the injured perfunctorily examined Pat, who gratefully acknowledged our help before he wandered off, unsteadily, to call his mother. Using my bottle of water I washed my hands of blood, letting it stream to the intricately patterned tile. I wiped up the puddles with the last of the paper towels, mindful of AIDS. I lit a cigarette.

I looked at the woman kneeling off to one side. We had forgotten to introduce ourselves, which we remedied now. Michelle Reuter. We tremulously agreed it was shaping up to be a bizarre morning and gave a little laugh. That was hardly an adequate description of the last twenty minutes. But there was little time to talk further—*boom!*—a second plane hit, and we grabbed each other.

The street was full of people running—some screaming, many crying. A woman was trying to reassure her school-age daughter. I watched the woman struggle to stay calm; it was obvious she was torn between comforting her child and trying to make a decision as to what to do next. I was immensely glad that my own son was not here, glad I didn't have to make decisions for Christopher and me.

There were voices fading in and out; I remember it being akin to having a receiver in my head that could be tuned into at will. I remember hearing others relaying information heard on newly purchased radios. Two planes. Both buildings. Evacuation. Fire crews. Jumpers. Don't go up to the towers. The Pentagon. I wasn't deathly afraid until that moment. I felt small and vulnerable, completely exposed. Were "they" bombing the city? Were other areas of New York being attacked? If "they" could hit the Pentagon, what were my chances of making it off this island alive?

In the time that followed until the South Tower collapsed, Michelle and I sat together on the porch of the Two Rector Street building, chain-smoking and talking about ourselves, why we were here today, cracking impossibly funny jokes despite the circumstances. She was twenty-four, a practicing Wiccan, an actress, a temp for American Express, beautiful, incredibly witty. I was thirty-four, a mommy, irreverent, an executive assistant extraordinaire with an active bullshit meter. We were both grateful to have someone to be with, to talk to, to share this incredibly tragic and ultimately historic event. We weren't alone anymore.

A massive rumbling began—we would find out later that it was the collapse of the South Tower—but at that moment, shielded from the Trade Center plaza, we didn't know what the ominous sound was. I know neither of us had a frame of reference for a sound that large. It reverberated in my chest, reminding me of the 1989 Loma Prieta earthquake in San Francisco. Michelle had lived through the Northridge quake a few years later, in Los Angeles. But nothing prepares you for a hundred-story building collapse.

We quickly moved toward the street but were pushed back almost instantly by the fleeing crowd. We did the best we could to avoid the herd but were turned around anyway after having made it about ten feet. Michelle's hand left mine, and I clung to the handicapped railing by the revolving doors. I prayed I wouldn't get crushed. I had a fleeting memory of that Ohio concert where fans were tragically crushed when the mob rushed the stage. Looking over my shoulder toward the street, I wondered what was happening and why the crowd was screaming.

Soon the yelling stopped. The silence ratcheted my fear to a new level. It seemed everyone had halted where they were. Why?

Then I felt it: wind—soft, filthy, and full of chunks, pattering against my back. It dropped into my clothing, matted my hair, stung my eyes, and choked my lungs. I couldn't breathe. I couldn't find Michelle. I had two thoughts: I don't want to die like this, and, Where is Michelle? I cracked my eyes open and immediately regretted it. They burned, and I couldn't see. From the darkness I heard Michelle's voice:

"Shira, I can't find you!"

"I'm right here! Take my hand—I don't want to die, Michelle! I want to go home and see my baby—today is his third birthday!"

"You will, I promise, you will." Michelle and I stood on opposite sides of the handicapped railing, struggling to breathe. The security force from my office building was trying to prevent people from coming in through the revolving doors; every time the doors opened, the dust cloud followed, choking the lobby with more thick brown dust. Eventually the people inside began filtering outside. They couldn't breathe any better in the lobby than they could on the street.

A woman of middle years, whose name I wish I knew, stood next to me. She began a soothing litany, telling us to cover our mouths and noses and breathe normally. In the terror of the moment, I'd forgotten my emergency training, so it hadn't occurred to me to simply pull my shirt over my face. I did this now, and the difference was immediate. I opened my eyes and made sure Michelle had her shirt over her face, too.

From the dark street came the sound of people: sane people, calm people, and obviously clean people. They emerged from the emergency security rooms inside an adjacent building, and they had come to get us.

A single male voice came from the gloom of the dusty street. "Link hands and follow me. Follow the sound of my voice." We linked and we followed, a large human chain into another world. We were escorted into a series of security rooms within each other. Each room we passed through went deeper into the guts of the building. These people were amazingly well prepared. There were cases of bottled water stacked along two of the walls, and on the center table stood boxes of rags. The management of this building must have taken the 1993 bombing seriously. We each took a bottle of water and a rag to clean and cover our faces. I rinsed my mouth out at the urging of one of our rescuers, spitting out the dust and hunks of building still filling it.

During the next hour or so, Michelle and I lay exhausted on an unfinished floor, listening to news radio and riding out the collapse of the second tower. We drank water, shared mints; Michelle gave me a barrette to keep the dirty hair from my face. Ultimately, though, we knew we needed to make a decision. Her apartment was on Staten Island, and a policeman in the lobby was letting people know there was one civilian ferry leaving Manhattan. We'd have to brave the street, something neither of us wanted to do, but we wanted more than anything to be able to leave this war zone.

Leaving the relative safety of that building took guts, real bravery. I did not want to go back outside, into yet another unknown. I didn't think I could deal with another manic onslaught. But we decided to head for the ferry terminal. She was used to taking the ferry to and from Staten Island. I had never taken the ferry in the three years I'd lived in New York, so Michelle would have to lead the way. We stepped out onto the street, which was littered with paperwork, scraps of metal, and maybe three inches of brown dust. The air had cleared somewhat but it still stank and was heavy with dust, so we kept the cloths tied around our faces. For the rest of my life I will remember how that dust tasted. It was sweet. I still shudder to think what it comprised. It was in our lungs and stomachs, and covered every inch of our skin. Mine had already started to burn, and I resisted the urge to scratch.

Along our route we stopped to use a pay phone. I called Roy's office and was disappointed he wasn't there. He had volunteered to assist the military police with lockdown procedures. I left a message with his boss that I was okay, and where we were heading. I gave him Michelle's home phone number. Then I left a quarter atop the payphone for the next person.

We were lucky to make it onto the ferry. There must have been five hundred people milling around waiting for that ferry to complete its docking routine. The gates opened, and out streamed grim-faced Staten Island and New Jersey firefighters. We wanted to leave the destruction zone—they were trying to get to it. The crowd erupted in spontaneous applause, loud and raucous.

An hour later, we arrived at the Staten Island Ferry Terminal, lucky to have made it out of Manhattan. A woman, filthy like we were, was crying and vomiting quietly along the exit route.

We stopped at a corner market, receiving odd and often pitying looks from the crowd. We looked like refugees. The manager of the store gave us hot, wet towels to clean ourselves. I bought a wine cooler and a can of lentil soup; Michelle grabbed her own can of soup and a bottle of Diet Coke. Neither of us was hungry, although it was after noon and we hadn't eaten. I guzzled the wine cooler.

I spent the night at her apartment, grateful, sad, exhausted. We cried a lot. We watched smoke billowing from Manhattan. We watched news stories and history being made. We each told our families via telephone what the other—a perfect stranger—had done on our behalf. I fell asleep on Michelle's bed and she generously let me have it for the night, even giving me a stuffed polar bear for comfort. Michelle spent the night on her foldout sofa, watching the news with her boyfriend late into the night. In the morning I fed her cat his Pounce, and received an excellent series of purrs for my trouble. It was hard to let Michelle sleep later than I had; I think I already felt we belonged to each other.

By the time the Verrazano Narrows Bridge had reopened, I was ready to go home. I wanted my husband, my baby whose birthday I had missed, my own clothes. But when it came time for Michelle and me to say goodbye, the parting was unbearable. We were safe, we were clean. We were fed and had our loved ones around us. Yet I remember it as the worst part of those two days, leaving my new friend behind.

In the years between then and now, Michelle and I recall that separation the same way: wrenching, worse than the fear and the dust. Wrong. Beyond sharing this intensely emotional disaster, Michelle and I discovered in each other a perfect bond, a soul-level knowledge of this person's substance and faults and aspirations, and an implicit trust and understanding that the other would always be there.

In the months that followed, Michelle and I phoned each other constantly. We got together as often as we could, after work in Manhattan, at home on weekends. We did the things many women friends do: cocktails, holiday shopping, movies. Michelle frequently ate dinner with us. I was thrilled for her to finally meet the baby to whom she had helped me get home.

The bond between us was palpable even before we learned, over time, all the particulars of each other's lives. We share the same outrageous sense of humor, a love for obscure movie lines, and an irreverence for most things sacred. Being friends with Michelle has shown me how much I had been missing during those very dry years regularly punctuated by moving from place to place. Our relationship has also allowed me to see beyond the limits of the introversion I'd carried with me from girlhood to a vivacity and spirit in my adult self that can no longer be hidden.

Sadly, my newfound relationship couldn't keep my family from being uprooted again. Roy and I had planned our New York exodus for July 2002. His job offered to take us to Arizona, and I was not going to turn down the opportunity to get away from the stress of the city for a while, though it broke my heart to consider leaving Michelle behind. Still, Michelle had long talked about making her own move, back to California, to be close to her family. After 9/11 she felt very alone in New York without them. Her job had disappeared with World Trade Center Building Number Seven, too. To fly home, she would have to sell her things. To rent a van to go one way would cost an outrageous sum.

I spoke to Roy, who seemed to understand implicitly, and we offered her the opportunity to come with us as far as Arizona when we moved. From there she could drive herself and her things the last eight hours to Los Angeles. Together, Roy, Christopher, Michelle, our Labrador retriever, Licorice, and I spent nine days driving cross-country with Michelle's things strapped to the roof of my new Honda minivan.

Now that Roy has retired from military service, we'll most likely be on the move again soon, probably back to the East Coast. We hope this will be the last time we move for many, many years, as we yearn to build something permanent for ourselves. I'll miss being in relatively close proximity to Michelle, though we'll see each other several times a year as we do now.

I know Michelle and I both initially worried that after September 11, the other would tactfully part company sometime later in the month or year. Technically we had no claim on one another. Yet she and I have remained close for almost three years now. In all this time, we have never questioned our immediate connection, both on 9/11 and afterwards.

In our relationship there is no jealousy, no arguing—only balance and respect. What are the odds of my meeting exactly this person under such circumstances? If such a thing as divine intervention can be believed in, or the existence of fairies and sprites making merry in the world could be proved, then Michelle and I agree that we were not just brought together but thrown together—directed, maneuvered, and blessed.

But really, we already knew each other. All that was left was to fill in some details.

Homegirls

Joshunda Sanders

Sure, there were things I wanted: a normal family, food on the table every night, a best friend. But I grew up isolated, and I didn't know how to ask.

Before I was born, my mother probably wanted the same things; instead, she endured constant loss. Two of her children ran away in their teens: One ended up in a group home, the other was struck and killed by a city bus when he was twelve. I was her baby girl and her last chance at motherhood. Her own mother died in a mental institution; her dad was gone, too. From the time Mom was thirteen, she had raised herself. Because her parents had left big emotional spaces in her life, she tried not to leave similar ones in mine. She thought she could make up for all the things we didn't have by telling me more than a few times a day that she loved me. "You're my best friend in the world," she'd say, lying in the dark of our apartment. "You're all I have."

I was silent when she said that to me. It was something she said all the time. I had spent most of my childhood taking care of her: I applied for Section 8 for her when I was eleven and filled out all the paperwork when it needed doing; I stole money from church collections when we ran out of money for bus fare. When she was too exhausted to cook, I rubbed her feet and bought us pizza slices for dinner. I took care of her the way I wanted her to take care of me.

She did have rare good days, when she would even sing while she cooked. She would kiss my forehead and leave me long notes before she left for work in the morning. But on her bad days, when the seams of her life refused to come together, she'd pound me with her fists or a curtain rod, whatever she could find. Curses and rants streamed from her mouth. I'd curl up in a ball until the storm passed. If I screamed for help or told someone—like I did when I was six and she inadvertently burned me with a straightening comb—I knew I'd be back in foster care and she'd have nobody, and neither would I. The least I could do was give her another chance, I thought. One day, she might change.

My distant relatives, whom we saw at infrequent reunions, whispered that she wasn't right in the head. When I got older, I thought maybe she had bipolar or post-traumatic stress disorder. But the truth is, I never knew and still don't. Mom refused to be diagnosed or take medication to regulate her moods.

All I knew was that all my life she couldn't keep a job for more than a few months. The rent was never paid on time, so we were always getting kicked out of one place or another, shuttling to and from shelters in the middle of long nights, wandering the streets like nomads.

By the time I was thirteen, I'd lived in four of New York City's five boroughs. The apartment we'd stayed at the longest was in the Bronx, where I had to run from my schoolmates every day to avoid being beat up. I was skinny and timid with no friends: perfect bait for bullies. Jocelyn, the thuggish Dominican girl with bony knuckles, took to chasing me on days when she had extra energy left over after school. Carlos, a Puerto Rican boy too fat to run for more than a minute, liked to sit his wide ass on my chest during recess until I cried asthma. I used to watch the clock and dash out of class every day at two seconds to three so I could rush through the front door and up the block to get a head start on whoever's turn it was to pummel me. It was a good thing none of them had library cards: You can't get past security at the West Farms New York Public Library without one.

I tried telling myself it didn't matter. Books were my company. Through their pages, I could live in the worlds of blue-eyed girls in two-story houses on sunny blocks with plush, manicured lawns—not in the real world of loud and musty subways skidding over streets, or window guards blocking my view of the horizon. If I never looked up from the page, I could live that imaginary life instead of the one I hated.

Still, school was my escape from home, my sanity. When school was out, I could keep the books with me—I sensed they might be catalysts to move me away from my broken home and neighborhood. When my sixth-grade teacher gave me an application for De La Salle Academy, an independent school dedicated to educating academically gifted but economically underprivileged children, I knew I had to apply.

So I took the test to get in, filled out the application, and dragged my mother to the interview. When I was accepted, I saw it as a sign from God. Maybe I could be different here. I could change my image, I could act cool, and the kids at this new school might be nice to me. After all, they were poor nerds, too.

When I arrived, I was a little disappointed to find that all the typical classroom hierarchies were still in place, in a way: The cool kids had gold-plated name chains and shoes for every day of the week; the real geeks were sometimes stinky, with bad breath, hungry eyes, and chapped lips. Everyone in between was just a blur to me: quiet, detached.

The older kids, the eighth graders, were the kings and queens of this junior high school. Half of them had started doing it the summer before; note-passing and crushes were things they were too grown for at fourteen. Most of the kids there had known each other since at least the year before, and in I walked, wanting to be liked and believing it was possible.

The teenage royalty aside, I did feel safe enough to develop a crush on a boy that first day, and decided that liking him would be enough for him to like me back. I passed him a poem in homeroom. He passed it back with a note at the bottom that read: "Deez Nuts."

I was crushed. Here I was trying to be cool and sweet, and already, my reputation as the psycho poet was making the rounds. Monique knew about it because, well, that guy was her boyfriend.

Monique was a petite Napoleon with a voice twice as big as her just-above-five-foot frame. Whenever she opened her mouth, a crowd leaned in to catch the words as they fell. When she walked into a room, shoulders back, hair done, and head up, you'd almost forget she was so little. There was no way not to know purple was her favorite color: Her favorite pen, a dozen of her shirts, and even her sneakers were grape-colored. I wasted the first half of seventh grade obsessed and jealous, understanding why Michael liked her over me. I hoped that eventually she would forget about me stalking her man for long enough to really get to know me. But I told myself we were too different. Sure, I was smart, but she was popular. It was the stuff of *Degrassi Junior High,* with more black people and less grass.

Monique's closest friend was Shanasia, a dark-skinned girl with slick, straight black hair she always wore pulled back in a ponytail. She was from Brooklyn and I decided immediately to hate her just for that. When she called me out for wearing high-water pants, my hatred only fermented. She and Monique had been friends since summer camp a few years back, and they were both Geminis. Sometimes I heard them talking to each other, laughing at somebody or something while they walked to the train station in their small tribe, me following with my hands stuffed in my pockets, listening to Mariah Carey on my old Walkman. I tried not to be too obvious about watching them so closely.

* * *

Halfway through seventh grade, we started having group therapy sessions at school—right around the time Mom and I were evicted from our fourth apartment and were living in a temporary shelter in Brooklyn. Monique and Shanasia were in my group. When I talked about my mom, described the apartments with no furniture, I watched Monique sit pensively, her glasses weighing on her tiny nose and her slanted brown eyes looking right at me.

At the end of one session, we were told to pair off for an assignment, and because she was sitting next to me, we became partners. When she said she would call me, I gave her a fake number. The night before we were supposed to report to the group again as a pair, I called her from a pay phone in the shelter lobby.

"Where are you calling me from?" she demanded.

"Outside," I said. I felt the questions she was about to ask in my gut, and I leaned against the pay phone, waiting. It was weird to hear her concern, but I didn't want her pity, and I didn't want to tell her more than she needed to know. In my other schools, only a few teachers had known about my home situation, and I never talked about it to anyone else. I certainly wasn't going to broadcast it to any of the two hundred kids at De La Salle and risk making myself an outsider again. Problem was, I'd always been a bad liar.

"What happened to the phone at your house?"

My first reaction was to tell her that it was disconnected. Then I thought of saying, "Maybe you wrote it down wrong." What came out was the truth: "I don't have a house."

It was the first time I'd said that to anyone not employed by the state or by a church. She paused for a long minute and asked me again where I was. I looked at the phone. The popular girl knew one of my best-kept secrets. As I wondered how she might use it against me, she invited me to her apartment to hang out and do our schoolwork. She lived in the Bronx, in the Webster projects. It looked like a war zone from the outside, with trash bags lining the front sidewalks and the back bordering a barren playground and spare basketball court.

This was where she lived? From the way she carried herself, I thought she probably lived in a condo like the one on *The Jeffersons*. Inside her apartment, it was a different scene. There were a plush carpet and chairs in the living room, and plastic green containers for food in the small, sun-filled kitchen. Framed pictures of her brothers and sister decorated the walls. It was so warm in there—they actually had heat—and it smelled like incense.

By the time I left, there wasn't much time to talk about the shelter where I was living. She told me I could call her, if I needed to. Whatever I needed. I was ecstatic.

And, in the tradition of real, genuine, and concerned friends, she told on me. Told our principal that she was worried, that I was commuting two hours on the train every morning from a homeless shelter. Next thing I knew, I was in his office with my mom, wondering how he found out. He touched my hand when he told me that Monique was the informant. As relieved as I was, I was also really pissed. It was my life and my suffering and who was she to tell anyone about it?

De La Salle's principal, Brother Brian, had us moved to a temporary-housing hotel not far from the school. He checked in with me every day to make sure I was okay. And each day I walked to school, I thought of what it meant that Monique had told. My indignation didn't last long. Hers was the first gesture of kindness from a friend I had ever received.

When I had the money, I called her every single day. I followed homegirl around everywhere, until she told me to give her space. She even got her twin brother and mom to tell me she wasn't home sometimes, just so I wouldn't call her five times a day. If none of that deterred me, she knew how to buy herself all the space she needed.

One day, for example, while we were at the library, she sat next to me and said, "You have a bit of an odor."

I looked up from the paper in front of me, silent.

"It's . . . it's kind of a urine smell."

"I live in a shelter, Mo. It's not like I want to smell like that."

"There are things you can do to help, you know, like making sure you wash your underwear really good and stuff like that," she started.

"Oh, yeah," I said, sarcastically, nodding my head. "Thanks for telling me."

There were times when I wasn't sure if she liked me just because she liked having someone around that she could fix. When her honesty stung, I'd skulk off into the corner with my wounded-pigeon strut and days would pass. Then, she'd have a bad day, someone would make fun of her thick glasses, or the acne on her face would make her feel ugly, and I'd ask her if she wanted to walk down the street and get some french fries. Over food, during our after-school walks, sometimes she opened up about feelings that her cool friends didn't always hear about.

No matter what we said to each other, I knew she wanted me to be better—and I wanted to be better because she was watching. I got the feeling that she wanted to be better, too—I just didn't know in what way.

She was the youngest in her family by a few minutes, and also being the smallest, she always yearned to be truly heard. Her mother was a substance-abuse counselor and raised four children with minimal help from their father. Two of Monique's siblings had gone to elite high schools and colleges, and she was expected to follow in their footsteps.

In the projects where she lived, she was the cute girl that all the boys around the way wanted to get with—but she had school on her mind, and she demanded that they respect her the way she demanded it of everyone else. When I arrived in her life, I think I was just a quirky distraction. But I gave her someone to talk to about the intersection of expectations people placed on her shoulders.

I had thought of her, at first, as the girl with everything. But while her mother always provided the best she could for Monique and her siblings, they weren't rich. They were just a normal family, getting by with what they had. Monique sometimes confided in me that she missed her dad and wished he'd never left. She hated the Bronx; she wanted a house of her own. I didn't always know what to say, except to tell her that one day she would be able to tell her dad exactly how she felt. Maybe one day she'd have the house she wanted and all those feelings would pass.

Every summer night after we graduated ended with her asking me, "Would you just get on the bus?"

It was my habit to leave her house and walk home past abandoned warehouses, under freeway underpasses, and the like. I was used to walking everywhere since I never had money for tokens—I had once walked the length of Manhattan with my mother. One time I slipped and told Monique, and it freaked her out that I was walking the 25 blocks in the dark. "I don't like the bus," I lied.

She'd give me a dollar and a quarter, walk with me to the bus stop, and wait to watch me until I got on. Really, I told her, she didn't have to stand there like I was a criminal.

"I know if I leave you'll just walk," she'd say, frowning.

By the end of the summer, I'd be able to walk to Queens, if I wanted: Monique was going to boarding school. We said we'd write, she said she'd be home for breaks and holidays, but it felt like she was leaving me behind.

Monique's leaving was made worse by my mom's feelings about our relationship. The closer I got to Monique, the more jealous my mother became. Her episodes weren't too bad at the time, and we had been living in the same apartment for more than two years. As I had for years, I still entertained thoughts of suicide in long quiet stretches between midnight and dawn, but I never got to stay with those thoughts for long before Monique would call to gossip or tell me she'd seen something really funny.

I was on the phone with her one night when my mother started in. "You're always on that damn phone," she said. "Get off the fucking phone."

I hung up and crawled into bed. The sky was silent and dark, except for a twinkling plane roaring through the sky. "Think you're so grown, got you a little girlfriend and shit," she sneered.

I muttered something back, pushing my mouth into my pillow. She climbed on top of me, her hands around my throat. "What did you say? *What?!* Speak up, you little bitch. I'll kill you! I'll *kill* you in here if you talk back to me." It felt like her hands would stay there forever, taking my breath. Finally, she let go of my neck. When she got off me, she started crying and said she didn't mean to hurt me. She told me she was my best friend. But it was too late.

When my mother left for work the next morning, I wrote her a goodbye letter. I packed a garbage bag of clothes and books and showed up on Monique's doorstep. She and her mother stared at me for a minute, then, without asking any questions, her mom took the bag, Monique gave me a fresh pillow, and they took turns telling me everything would be fine.

That weekend, two weeks before she left for boarding school, Monique and I would lie side by side in her twin bed, talking for hours in the dark about the women we wanted to be one day: strong, together, free to buy all the clothes and good things we wanted. She wanted to be an occupational psychologist; I didn't know what that meant. I wanted to be a fashion designer and a teacher and a writer— whichever happened first. We'd get married, maybe, and have babies.

"Will you be my maid of honor?" she asked me.

"Sure," I said. "I guess. I don't like marriage, I don't think."

"You don't have to like it, you just have to show up," Monique said.

We went to a slumber party and stayed up all night in our pajamas eating ice cream and forgetting the world. After a week of my mom calling Monique's house every day, then showing up to curse out the whole family, I went back to my house. It felt different to me. I felt stronger knowing that I could run if I had to, because there was some- where to go.

When the summer was over, the sky poured down thick gray rain- drops as I walked to Monique's house to watch her pack her first big suitcase. I don't remember saying goodbye when she left for boarding school. But I remember understanding that the danger of loving someone, anyone, meant that sometimes they would leave—and that any real friend would be able to let her go.

That first year apart was the hardest. I didn't have long-distance phone service, so I hardly ever spoke to Monique—but we did write letters and hang out during vacations.

I was attending a Catholic school in the Bronx. I was the new girl again, but I didn't care because I had bigger things to worry about. I joined the track team, found a boyfriend, and started coming into my own. I had developed a shaky confidence, but it felt real. And it made me feel big—big enough that the next time my mother tried to beat me, I grabbed her wrist and threw her on my bed. "I'm bigger than you now," I told her. "You should think twice about hitting me all the time." The bully era was over. She backed down and wept.

It was a bittersweet triumph. I knew that as much as I had changed, my mother had not and she probably wasn't going to. I would have to leave her. I applied to boarding school. She was pissed off that I was abandoning her. I left anyway.

In the elite boarding-school world, my schoolmates seemed to like me because I was "keepin' it real." I was authentic ghetto—with Timberland boots to match my hard-luck story. I couldn't be the overly eager, mousy girl anymore: I was quiet, brooding, and distant, and surrounded by the wealthy daughters of aristocrats, lawyers, and surgeons, most of them white. I wrote poetry about them, tucked myself away in the library where I sometimes found black women who wrote my world into existence: Maya Angelou, Ntozake Shange, Audre Lorde. Their words, to me, were a continuation of conversations I'd had with Monique.

I felt like an outsider that first year, which is what I wrote to Monique sometimes. She felt it, too. "But," she wrote, "look where we had come from, and look where we are." When she sent frustrated letters, I wrote her words of encouragement and sometimes poems to cheer her up. Our connection gave us both perspective and enough emotional ammunition to keep going when it seemed like we were too far out of our leagues. I started to feel free. I posed in my dorm-room mirror as a revolutionary poet, a sister girl, a retro-'70s diva. I pierced my nose, started wearing head wraps, and questioned my sexuality. Four hours north of the Bronx, with my mother's infrequent calls and no one else besides her and Monique to check in on me, I felt like I could become whoever I wanted to be—for real this time.

In the back of my mind, I knew I only had one thing to lose: What if I changed too much and Monique didn't like the woman I'd turned into? I told myself that if Monique could love me poor, geeky, and smelly, she could love me as a confused bohemian black chick with too much time to wander by creeks and tall trees.

Three years of hard work later, I applied to ten colleges and chose Vassar. But my demons started haunting me again once I finished my two-hundred-page thesis: I started panicking about my uncertain future.

"What if I don't get a job and I have to go back to live with my mom . . . or what if, after all this, I end up homeless again?" I ranted. "All this work, Mo, for nothing. I'm so tired."

"You're going to be fine," she said, wearily. I'd called her at two in the morning. It was the home stretch before college graduation, so I should've been elated. But I was hyped up on Dunkin' Donuts coffee and nicotine; my body was exhausted but my mind was jittery.

More than my future career was on my mind. During my sophomore year, my mother had moved across the street from campus after being evicted from our apartment in the Bronx. I sometimes refused to see her, but she would show up anyway, bringing me things I didn't need that she'd gotten at her job at Stop 'N Shop: chicken wings, toilet paper, soap. Even while I was writing my thesis, she would show up, just to say hello.

"Girl, listen to me," said Monique. "You're not going to be homeless again, okay? Go to sleep. You'll feel better after you get some rest. You're buggin' right now."

Monique was always right. She graduated from Cornell with a degree in business; I graduated from Vassar with a liberal arts degree. She went to work for Phillip Morris. I took a journalism fellowship, which meant I would be moving to four different cities for the next two years to work as a newspaper reporter. Monique cheered; my mother whined.

"Are you ever coming back?" my mom asked when I went to visit her.

"Of course," I said. "I'll come back to visit."

"I don't know what I'll do without you," she answered. "I guess I'll have to just deal with it, huh? You're growing up."

"Ma, I've been grown."

"Is Monique going, too?" Mom had taken to asking about Monique every time we talked, ever since a conversation we'd had in which I explained to her that even though the girl was my best friend, it didn't mean that I didn't love my mother. She could not be replaced, I assured her—she was one of a kind.

"No, she'll be in New York," I answered.

"Oh, so you're coming back cuz she's here," she said. "Make sure you call me, okay? I'll send you money. Go to church, find a good church down there." My mom grabbed my face and gave me a sloppy kiss on the cheek. "You're special, baby girl. God bless you."

Now that Monique and I are in the "real world" and in our mid-twenties, we know firsthand that friends don't just show up. Life almost always feels crazed, like there's never time to really have the freedom we used to have—but as much as everything around us has changed, we still have each other.

It took ten years, but I've finally realized the power of giving and receiving in friendship. I've learned how to accept help, how to be the consistent, comforting voice in another person's world without depriving myself of those same things.

When Monique and I talk, I know she's my homegirl for life. She stopped me from running away when things could've spiraled out of control. As I grew strong in our friendship, I helped her make sense of relationships and situations that threatened to throw her off track. When she decided that she hated Phillip Morris, she became a teacher back at De La Salle. When she called me in trepidation, I reassured her that she was such a great communicator, the kids were going to love her. I also said something she'd said to me countless times before: "You're going to be fine."

The Garbo Girl

by Molly Kiely

the Garbo Girl

MOLLY KIELY '04

I live in the desert in a rural neighbourhood with a boyfriend I adore. He's my favourite person ...but I have few friends besides. I am a hermit.

A recluse.

A sophisticated loner.

• • •

I tend to live in a world of my own creation. I like to be alone; I can converse with trees and flowers and chat up birds unselfconsciously.

I'm a happy person and I don't dislike people. I enjoy sparkling conversation and dinner parties and intense talks. I am a compassionate girl.

Yet, I feel no need to agree, conform, or sympathize.

Women tend to sympathize and confide in each other and offer emotional support. I don't have it in me. Body issues? Eat properly, exercise. Relationship issues? Tell them. Money issues? Be frugal. Yeah, yeah, Bush can kiss my ass — they all can. Look, can we go to an art museum? How 'bout a Hike?

I realize I come across as distant and aloof. I don't need my feelings, opinions, or tastes validated and I forget that other people might. That said—

... can't we just enjoy this sunny afternoon?
...the pretty flowers?
...this lovely viognier?
• • •

I know I'll be one of those eccentric old ladies in a colourful cottage who talks to birds and arranges her dolls for tea at three 'cos it's fun, not because she thinks they're real (altho' by then, who knows)

... and that's perfectly fine by me.

Another Mother

Ayun Halliday

That first year in the playground, the year my daughter, Inky, learned to walk and then talk, I didn't know anyone's last name, though we saw the same people day after day, dressed for rain or snow or the swelter of a New York City heat wave. East Village apartments are overwhelmingly small, and walls close in quickly when you spend every waking hour with the young of the species.

The playground in Tompkins Square, while filthy and subject to whatever the weather was dishing out, was convivial. The casually friendly vibe was not unlike the neighborliness I took for granted growing up in Indiana. The major difference was that the setting was new to me and vastly improved by the presence of black people, French people, tattooed people, Korean people, gay people, heavily tattooed people, borderline crazy people—all of whom had children. I didn't know anyone else with children, not in New York. What's more, these parents lived in my New York, the New York of tiny apartments, unreliable heat, and low-budget artistic striving. All of us were trying to figure out how we could reconcile motherhood with the people we'd been before the babies came along to change everything. I doubt I would have fit in so well on the playgrounds of the Upper East Side, where rumor had it uniformed nannies refused to mix with the few parents who ventured onto their turf.

In retrospect, hanging out in Tompkins Square was a little like hanging out in the parking lot after high school was dismissed for the day, bitching about teachers, parents, and homework, endlessly vamping on such interesting topics as who's going to ask who out, who got suspended for having a pot seed in her purse. You know, nothing earthshaking, but proof that you are a part of something, a community. With the playground crew, I could be who I'd always been, a great relief given mainstream culture's mania to desexualize, clean up, and otherwise limit mothers of young children. I could also be a mother, one of many. I felt much more relaxed and happy hanging out in Tompkins Square than I did whenever I attempted to shoehorn myself and the kid into my old life.

My old cronies were as funny as ever, bursting with engaging anecdotes about their ongoing child-free lives in Manhattan's many bars, hole-in-the-wall theaters, and mental health facilities, but I found it increasingly hard to give them my full attention. I was too busy crawling around their apartments on my hands and knees, securing their extension cords and protecting their alphabetized CD collections from my marauding child. When they made plans to go out on the town, I was shit out of luck. So while few of my newly minted, alfresco friendships extended beyond the confines of the playground, those mothers—and some honorary stay-at-home fathers, too—meant the world to me at that time. So what if I didn't know their last names? I knew the children's names, what everyone's winter coat looked like, and how potty-training was going in each household. I knew the circumstances under which many of the children had been born, often in great detail, since we had nothing better to do and certainly nowhere better to be.

For hours, we chewed the fat under the incongruously lovely

maples overhanging the baby swings. I learned that Harry was born in a taxi on the way to the hospital. Lucas refused to come out at the birthing center, so his mother was transferred to St. Vincent's, just like I had been. Viola was living in a rice field in Bali when Jessye started to come. I was particularly interested in this story because I had traveled to Bali with both my husband, Greg, and with one of his predecessors.

Whenever Viola talked about Bali, I skipped along down Memory Lane, happily reminded of the full life I had led before embarking on a different sort of full life thanks to a shoddily inserted diaphragm. As news of Viola's labor started to sweep through the grapevine of Ubud, the tourist hotspot in which she lived, her house filled up with joyous women—"Ooh, just the kind of birthing experience I would have liked to have," I interjected—but then things started going haywire. Her husband had to race down a dirt track on his moped with Viola clinging on for dear life, just to get to a place where they could find better transportation to the only hospital on the island. Viola told me that she had named her son after her mother, and that now she wanted to get back to Bali because she hated the cold weather. She got her wish. The family scraped enough money together to return to Bali just as the rest of us had to break out the snowsuits.

Over that winter, I got to know the others better, even learned a few full names: Anna Brackett, Char Daigle, Nancy Simko, Binda Colebrook, Rose Papallardo, and Chara McGill. I saw the insides of their apartments and attended their children's birthday parties. I started a zine about my life as an East Village mother.

Then warm weather returned, and with it came Viola. I didn't know they were back until I ran into her husband, Oded, coming out of the playground. "Hey, look who's here," I cried, as he clicked his fingers as if to say, "Oh yeah, right, you." At his suggestion, we exchanged phone numbers. Along with their New York info, he gave me a card printed with their phone number and address in Bali in case we ever made it back to Indonesia. He apologized for forgetting my name.

He had remembered Inky's and that, we agreed, was the important thing. We made noise about getting the kids together for a play date, but in truth I preferred the easy serendipity of running into each other on the playground. That was where I enjoyed the others' company best, and besides, sooner or later, everybody was bound to show up.

Oded called a week later, just as we were heading out the door to yet another two-year-old's birthday party. When I told him of our plans, he asked if they could come along. Nervously, I said that I wished I could say yes, but the party was taking place on a beach way out in Brooklyn, past Coney Island. There wasn't room for four adults and two car seats in my husband's old Dodge Shadow. I hung up relieved and somewhat amazed that I hadn't put myself in the position of bringing three uninvited guests, which struck me as presumptuous, especially since I barely knew our hosts. They were under enough pressure already. At these affairs, the adults tended to stand around awkwardly, making dull observations about the children. People who were freewheeling and familiar in the playground, myself for example, tended to clam up outside the magic circle of Tompkins Square. I still haven't figured out why that is. Did you ever meet a kid you were wild about at summer camp, only to discover that you found it difficult to think of things to say to each other when she came to spend a weekend with your family later that same year? Maybe the presence of the birthday child's parents' "real" friends—people who'd known them since college or high school, the best man at the wedding, the bass player from the father's band—was intimidating.

Nonetheless, when Inky's birthday loomed a few weeks later, I invited every playground crony whose name I knew, even the ones who could barely sit up unassisted, in addition to my "real" friends. I've got this thing about inclusiveness, stemming back to elementary school when young hostesses used the old "there were only ten paper plates in the pack" line on Unfortunate Classmate Number Eleven. Greg and I couldn't squeeze more than four guests into our apartment, but that was okay since the party was in the playground. It was 102 degrees in the shade, but the only ones unused to the heat were my childless "real" friends, whom I correctly expected would decamp for air-conditioned locations after putting in their obligatory appearances. Everybody else stayed for the duration. Jessye's folks said they would come but they didn't.

Greg later ran into Viola in the playground; she apologized, saying they'd decided to head to a friend's place upstate to escape the heat. "Who could blame them?" I said, wondering why none of my friends had weekend cabins in the Catskills or the Hamptons.

"She has a present for Inky," Greg said.

"That's nice." I had put "no presents" on the invitation. I wanted everybody to come, but I felt funny asking them to shell out hard-earned dough on an acquaintance from the playground. Also, I was terrified by the prospect of junking up our minuscule apartment with a bunch of Teletubbies and plastic toys. Instead, I asked everyone to bring a picture of a monkey to paste into a scrapbook. I'm so creative.

"She says she'll stick it in her bag to give to you the next time she sees you. What's her name again?"

"Viola."

"Right. We had a pretty interesting conversation about Indonesian politics. She's really knowledgeable about the situation over there."

"Great. I'm glad you found someone you enjoyed talking to on the playground, honey." For many reasons, Greg's identity was not tethered to the Tompkins Square playground's social swirl the way mine was. I was a hardcore regular and proud of it. I liked to feel involved, keep tabs on the others in the hope that they were keeping similar tabs on me. When it rained, I watched the sky anxiously for signs of clearing so that we could go to the playground, even if Inky was content to amuse herself indoors. It's like I had to hurry back to Brigadoon, before it and all its inhabitants vanished in the mist, leaving me alone with my child.

"You should call her," Greg said, flopping down on the rag rug–covered

massage table that served as our couch. "She wants to get the kids together for a play date."

Before I got around to picking up the phone, Viola started keeping
regular playground hours, the way she had the previous summer,
when Jessye was still crawling. She explained that she'd finally gotten him back on East Village time. I nodded sympathetically, remember-
ing how when we flew to Los Angeles, jet lag had roused Inky two
hours before dawn every day for a week. We told each other how glad
we were to have Jessye's naps in sync with Inky's, because it meant seeing more of each other. I wouldn't have to call after all.

I thought Viola looked tired. She had cut off the glamorous braids
she'd sported when we met. I wondered if she was depressed. I knew
she hated being in New York, but I didn't like to take the conversation in that direction because I loved New York. I didn't want to hear myself running it down just to cheer her up. She rarely joined in when the
rest of us got going on our landlords or the futility of our college degrees.
Maybe she felt awkward because she'd missed out on six months'
worth of bonding, those times when the whole gang crammed into one
of the larger apartments to escape the sleet, slurp coffee, break up
battles over the possession of Tinky Winky, and ultimately leave our
hostess with several Ziploc bags' worth of Cheerios crushed underfoot. Those gatherings came the closest to replicating the playground
vibe indoors, when Rose or someone would marshal whoever happened to be around when it started coming down, transferring us en
masse to a drier location. In an effort to make her feel included, I for-
mally introduced—in some cases reintroduced—Viola to the mothers I
liked best. Sometimes she'd rise to the occasion, throwing her head back
to laugh the way I remembered, shaking her head vigorously at the folly
of raising small children. It was good to see her acting like her old
self, but mostly she was quiet.

I felt sorry for her when Jessye whaled on her with a small plastic hammer. It was clear she didn't have the energy to fend him off. "Hey there, thuggy-pants, quit banging on your mama!" I cajoled, taking care not to seem like I was disciplining another woman's child. "You don't want to break her, do you?"

"It's okay," she sighed, shielding her face with the back of her hand. "If I take it away, he'll just get me with his shovel or a drumstick. He can turn anything into a hammer."

In solidarity, I made some crack about the little killers trouncing us big monkeys and refrained from voicing relief that Inky didn't get her jollies from beating me up.

Once, a childless friend of Viola's showed up to take over for a few hours. Viola looked like a new woman as she grabbed her shoulder bag from the handles of Jessye's stroller and made a beeline for the iron gate. I felt a bit wistful seeing her with her "real" friend and a lot wistful that it wasn't me rushing off to see a movie all by myself at the Village East. I was still mooching around the playground when she returned a few hours later, radiant, chatty, eagerly giving a big thumbs-up to the screen adaptation of Toni Morrison's *Beloved,* starring Oprah Winfrey. "Ooh, now I'll have to get Greg to watch Inky so I can see it," I lied. I wished she had seen *Happiness* instead, a misanthropic film that I had loved about a pedophile dad. It was the only movie I'd seen in months, one that I would have enjoyed discussing at length on the playground. Oprah Winfrey, for God's sake—not that I begrudged Viola her right to enjoy a Hollywood vehicle unusually commanded by black women. I still haven't seen it. Maybe it's the masterpiece Viola said it was. I hope it is.

"Oprah Winfrey is so powerful," she intoned, flexing her biceps with relish.

"Mmm," I agreed.

July was almost over when Naomi's mother, Zoe, called me from the playground on a borrowed cell phone. It was the first time we'd ever spoken on the telephone and it took me a minute to get a handle on who was calling. Her words tumbled out in a rush, her voice an octave higher than usual. "Can you tell me your friend's name, Jessye's mother? She just collapsed in the playground and nobody here knows her! Do you know where she lives or her phone number or anything?"

I reached for my address book. Miraculously, it was right by the phone, not buried under a pile of zines, bills, and toys. I gave her the number I had copied from the business card Oded had given me. I spelled his surname, but said I doubted it was the same as Viola's. They were married, though. I remembered Viola telling me they had decided to tie the knot when they found out she was pregnant. Zoe sounded like she was crying. The paramedics were there. I asked if she thought I should come. Inky was expected at her best friend Abby's in twenty minutes. "Can you come get Jessye?" she replied. "Oh god. Oh god. It's really bad."

I can't deny that it was somewhat flattering, Zoe's supposition that I was a more appropriate choice to keep an eye on Jessye than she was. I placed so much importance on being involved with our playground community—well, here was proof that I was. I tore out of the apartment so fast I forgot to put shoes on Inky. The rockabilly kids who ran the vintage store on our block were surprised to see me moving so swiftly; usually I crept along at Inky's pace, back and forth to the playground at least twice a day. They called out a cheery greeting, and I returned it in kind. What was up with that? If one of my "real" friends had been lying unconscious in Tompkins Square, I would have barreled right past them. On the other hand, I have a tendency to remain doggedly optimistic in the face of disaster, certain that nothing can go really wrong as long as I act like everything's okay.

When I got there, it was, as Zoe had said, really bad. Viola was on her back by the tire swing, and as I wrenched open the gate, the crowd of onlookers burst into applause because the paramedics had gotten her heart beating again. I tacked toward Jessye, parked thirty feet away in his stroller, sitting stoically in a disposable diaper and tiny leather sandals. "I can take him back to my place. We live right around the corner on 9th Street," I told a policewoman standing nearby. "He knows me." I smiled confidently as if this were the absolute truth. Having taken a moment to size me up, the policewoman asserted that there was no way anyone would release Jessye into my care. "We'll have to take him into Family Services if we can't locate the father."

Apparently, when you stop breathing in Tompkins Square, if you're young and you're black, you're automatically considered a drug addict.

"I know his father," I stammered, pulling out my address book with shaking hands. "I'm a friend of the family!" Grudgingly, the police-woman said that if I wanted, Inky and I could accompany Jessye wherever they ended up taking him. Of course I wanted. The imperative to be really involved was no longer a matter of personal preference. I was Jessye's connection to his mother in a way no well-meaning emergency room nurse or desk sergeant could be. What would I think if I collapsed in Tompkins Square and the other mothers let Family Services carry Inky away?

Using another borrowed cell phone—I had to be shown how to use it—I left a message for Oded on their home machine. "Hi, it's Ayun, Inky's mom, from the playground. Uh, Viola got sick in the playground, but I think she's going to be okay. The paramedics are here and they'll probably be taking her to the hospital. Jessye's fine. He's with me and he's welcome to stay with us for however long. No trouble at all. So I think we're going to end up back at my apartment, but listen, if you get this message, call Greg at work and he'll be able to put you in touch with me in case we're not home when you call. Okay?" After I supplied the address and Greg's work number, I had the guy who owned the cell phone dial Greg at work so I could tell him what was going on.

Over by the tire swings, the paramedics took out shock paddles. "Okay, people, let's go!" a burly policeman shouted, herding everyone toward the south exit. "This playground is closed as of now! Everybody out!" Inky and I stayed abreast as the policewoman pushed Jessye's stroller toward the ambulance just outside the gate. I grabbed Zoe and had her scribble her number in the back of a matchbook-sized Beatrix Potter book I pulled from my pocket. I promised that I'd call as soon as I knew anything. She squeezed my hand and wished me luck. They put us in a squad car just as Viola was wheeled through the crowd on a gurney. Her eyes, though open, were vacant. Jessye didn't notice his mother sailing past him, above the sea of adult knees populating his line of vision. He had a hell of a good time in that squad car, though, yanking on the grill and climbing onto the back ledge with Inky. I let them run amok, anything to keep them happy and distracted.

The ambulance took off with Viola, but the squad car remained parked on Avenue A for an eternity as the emergency personnel left at the scene completed their paperwork. Through the open window, I listened to the policewoman I'd spoken with chatting with a colleague. "Overdose," I heard her say. I wish I had confronted her, but I was worried about upsetting Jessye's apple cart. I'm not a believer, but thank God he came with me willingly. Thank God. Maybe he did recognize me, or more likely, Inky. I strove to keep it light, keep him entertained, went into peekaboo overdrive.

Just before we got underway, a hunky young fireman asked if he could hitch a ride, crowding into the backseat in his rubber pants. "Aren't you hot?" I asked. He laughed and told me that he was. "So, in your professional opinion, I mean, seeing as how you go to a lot of emergencies, do you think she's got a chance of making it?" He looked at me, shook his head apologetically, and turned to gaze out the window. After we dropped him at the firehouse on 14th Street, we doubled back to the Ninth Precinct, the one whose facade I used to see as a child in Indiana, watching *Barney Miller*. A motherly desk sergeant offered to give the children roast beef sandwiches and big glasses of milk. I tried to remember if Viola had ever mentioned anything about being vegetarian. I wondered if I should offer to nurse Jessye, if between all the mothers in Tompkins Square, we could keep him supplied with breast milk for just a little bit longer.

A detective escorted us to a room on the second floor where we might be "more comfortable." I suspected we were the only people in the history of the Ninth Precinct ever to have blown soap bubbles in the interrogation room. Some provocatively dressed ladies locked in a pen at the end of the corridor were quite taken with the children, curious as to what we were doing there, but a uniformed officer told them to cool it. I called Abby's mother, Anna, to tell her we wouldn't be coming to play, and she swung by with fruit, toys, and a book about trucks. "I thought maybe it's something a boy would be interested in," she said, looking very sad. I read that book over and over, hamming it up lest my charge grow bored and start looking around for his mama.

When Jessye started to shiver in the air conditioning, I rooted through the plastic bag I'd found hanging from the handles of his stroller. It was filled with clothes from Jane's Exchange, the consignment store on Avenue A where we all shopped. I tried to pick out the T-shirt Viola would have liked best before deciding that we would have liked the same one, the orange one. The receipt was in her purse, along with some mousetraps from the hardware store and a coin purse containing a few bucks. Nothing with her last name on it. I let the cops take a look, to prove there was no drug paraphernalia. I tried to remember how my day had started. Like Viola's last hours, it had been unremarkable. I wondered if Viola ever idly imagined possible scenarios regarding her own death. I did, and it never involved a casual buddy from the playground sitting in the police station with my eighteen-month-old, reading the receipts in my purse like runes. Feeling a bit melodramatic, I silently paged Viola with a message not unlike the one I'd left on the answering machine. *Hi, Viola, it's Ayun and I just want you to know that Jessye is safe here with me and I'll get him to Oded and everything is going to be just fine and you were a beautiful woman and we'll all miss you and. . . .*

I looked up as the detective ushered in Jessye's aunt, a short white woman a couple of years older than me. "Actually, I'm Oded's ex-sister-in-law," she said, taking a hit off a bottle of Rescue Remedy. "We live in Oregon. We're just visiting this week. My kids and I are staying on their couch. We were out sightseeing when you called. I got your message off the machine when we got back. Your husband told me where to find you." I nodded, amazed that my hastily thrown together plan had worked. "So, um, how bad is she, do you think?"

I told her in as few words as possible, not wanting to telegraph anything to Jessye. We talked about how to find Oded. She said that he was working with a crew restoring a cathedral, but she didn't know which one. Then we talked about the East Village and her farm in Oregon, because we weren't sure what we had in common besides her ex-brother-in-law's wife, who couldn't be spoken of casually. After half an hour, we decided that she should go to Beth Israel, where Viola was, and that Inky and I would follow later with Jessye.

Shortly thereafter, the detective reappeared to tell me I was free to go. "I just got off the phone with the hospital. I'm sorry to have to tell you this, but your friend didn't make it. We've located the husband. We'll send a car for him."

"Does he know?" I asked.

"No, no. Only that his wife's at Beth Israel and we need him to come there."

Feeling as though I should hurry, I hustled downstairs with the children and the stroller. The detective authorized another police car to drive us the ten blocks to the hospital. "I'm so sorry for your loss," a young patrolman drinking coffee on the stoop offered. The cop who was driving us echoed his sentiments. It must be scripted.

"We were playground friends," I explained, not realizing that from the officer's point of view, it was far preferable to deliver the police force's condolences to someone who wasn't wildly incapacitated with grief.

Inky fell asleep in the emergency room while we were waiting for Oded. Jessye's aunt took the stroller for a few laps through the little park adjoining the hospital. I didn't want to let him go, but of course her claim to him was greater than mine. A scrub-suited intern with a South African accent came out to tell me that she had been part of the team who worked on Viola when she was brought in. "I just want you to know we did everything we could. Cracked her chest. We gave her heart massage for much longer than we ordinarily would. I'm sorry." I couldn't help it. I started crying because Inky was asleep and Jessye was gone and Viola was dead and the intern was so nice.

Jessye and his aunt came back. We paced. Through the window, we noticed Oded getting out of a car that had pulled to the curb. Rather than having come with the policeman who'd been sent to fetch him, he'd accepted a ride from a coworker. I saw him get out of the passenger side, then stoop down to wave, smiling as he called out his thanks to the driver. His ex-sister-in-law rushed out to intercept him, steering him toward the park between the hospital and Second Avenue. His friend started to drive off, then thought better of it and pulled over again. After a few minutes, I stood up and carried Inky outside. She woke up crying and almost immediately threw up all over herself.

Oded's friend gallantly handed me a T-shirt from the backseat of his car to swab her down. "It's okay," he assured me. "I'm a father myself." Apologizing profusely, I gave him back his soiled T-shirt, thinking that the last thing any of us needed was for this situation to be made any more complicated and horrible, courtesy of a barfing toddler. Jessye's aunt came back and the three of us stood around, stealing sidelong glances at Oded, who sat in the park with Jessye in his lap. After a few minutes he stood and headed back toward the emergency entrance, carrying Jessye in his arms. The expression in his eyes was singular, animal. The way he stared at me, I wasn't sure if he knew who I was, but then he called Inky by name, caressing her head. In her vomitous state, she wanted nothing to do with anyone other than Mommy. I hoped that wouldn't hurt him. I hoped he wouldn't notice how badly she reeked.

"You were with her?" Oded asked me.

"Not right when it happened. Naomi's mother, Zoe, called me to come. She said Viola was pushing Jessye on the tire swing and then somebody noticed her lying on the ground. I'll find out more from her for you."

He squeezed my shoulder, already looking over my head. "I think I should go in to Viola now." Oh god, this was horrible beyond belief. I wondered what kind of morning they had had, whether she'd been awake when he left for work.

"Oded, if there's anything I can do. . . . I can watch Jessye. Whatever you want." He waved over his shoulder, not turning around. His friend offered to give us a lift home, but I preferred to walk. It was only six blocks. Have I mentioned that it was a beautiful day? Hot but gorgeous, with a cloudless sky, and at that hour, First Avenue was thronged with people coming home from work, eager to get out of their office clothes so they could go out for margaritas or whatever. With every person I passed, I thought how strange it was that they didn't know what had happened to Viola, to Jessye and Oded, and, to a much lesser extent, me.

When I got back to our flat, I told Greg everything that had transpired, starting with Zoe's frantic call. As he listened, he made a pot of macaroni for Inky. It seemed bizarre that we were still required to feed her, to bathe her, that everybody's life but Viola's—and, of course, Oded's—had to go on as usual. I called Zoe. I called Anna. I returned a call to a "real" friend of Viola's who somehow had gotten our number, possibly from one of Oded's ex-sister-in-law's kids. When she answered, I mispronounced her name and she was brisk, thinking me a telemarketer. Once we'd cleared that up, she demanded to know how Viola was, as if expecting a funny story involving a roller skate and a broken ankle. In the split second before I replied, I tried to weigh the options, to tell or not to tell. Should she call Viola's apartment and ask to speak to Jessye's aunt? I told her. I told her and she screamed like a bad actress in a bad movie, except that this was real. She was one of Viola's best friends. Tearfully, she told me that she would leave immediately to be by Oded's side. I washed the macaroni pot and gave Inky a bath.

The talk in the playground wasn't so much of Viola but of Jessye, how he was doing, who was taking care of him, what he understood. A couple of women who knew about me going with Jessye to the police station tried to give me the hero treatment, and although I'm usually happy to keep trotting an anecdote out until there's nobody left to hear it, I made sure I was quite clear about my modest role in the events surrounding Viola's death. I was the pragmatic housewife in white ankle socks and an apron, lending a hand when the neighbors were burned out of their home during the Blitz. Three hours from start to finish. Viola would have done the same for me.

"God, it hurts to think he won't remember her at all," the other mothers said when I told them what Oded had told me about Jessye asking once or twice for Mama before peacefully accepting his father's explanation that Viola had gone to live in the clouds. "I mean, can you imagine?" they asked, biting their lips as they watched their own children frolic and fight. "He won't remember his mommy!" That was the thing they all said, whether they'd known Viola or not. Beneath the lazy banter and the birth stories and the Veggie Booty, that was our primary connection. We were all killing ourselves taking care of children so little they wouldn't remember us if we were struck dead, no matter how achingly we loved them. And that was something to be glad for, should such an event come to pass, because otherwise they'd be screeching and throwing themselves on the floor, refusing to go anywhere with anyone but the one they can't have.

I got to know Viola much better after she died, thanks to her "real" friends, a warm, international bunch who gave her several incredible send-offs, kindly including me in all of them. At one, they gave out a large program, containing many photos—Viola graduating from high school, Viola dancing with the Urban Bushwomen, Viola looking quite the hottie in Bali, bending over the newborn Jessye, clowning around in her East Village kitchen. I was extremely glad to be given this keepsake. I'd already gone through my playground photos, dozens of snapshots in which Nancy or Chara or one of the others would turn up, slightly out of focus, caught unawares behind the child subjects. I thought maybe I'd find I'd gotten lucky, that Viola would have wandered into one of my backgrounds, but no. A couple of Jessye, drooling. God, he was the drooliest kid I ever met; even his mother said so. Just one of the little things I remember. It's strange to think that I remember more about Viola than her son ever will. These memories are small enough to fit in a teacup, but it's a teacup I'll carry with me for the rest of my life, my memento of someone who matters to me because she is gone, who might have become a "real" friend had she recovered, had both of us lived through those three hours.

Ordinary Gifts

Lauren Bower Smith

I am on my way back to Ouagadougou, the capital of Burkina Faso, West Africa, my own temporary residence and the home of my friend Rasmata. It is a summer evening. Though most of the boys and cattle have gone home, one or two young villagers are still weaving their way through the long grass to dinner. It is too dark to see them clearly, and they don't waste lamp oil or flashlight batteries on such a familiar path, but I sense their presence. Sometimes a narrow silhouette appears in the headlights, or a woman calls to a boy from the other side of the darkness. It is a scene of great tranquility, but it is a scene of shadows and suggestions only—a three-dimensional world seen through a two-dimensional lens. This is what it's like to talk to Rasmata. I get only hints and glimpses, but I know she is there, whole and vital.

I have traveled to Burkina Faso twice in the last two years: the first trip a three-week stay with my husband and daughter in tow; the second a three-month stay, one month with my family and two without. I made these journeys in order to visit my Burkinabé family-in-law and to work on a book of interview essays portraying West Africans affected by the AIDS epidemic, both those infected by the virus and those who have lost family members to the disease. Six members of my husband's extended family have died of AIDS, so the personal and the professional are deeply entwined for me. My work in Burkina Faso is partly a way of mourning and partly a way of facing the evil that has touched my family, wounding my husband and my American daughter, who asks why so many of her cousins have died.

Rasmata was one of my interview subjects, a market woman with whom I did not share a language. Our friendship was improbable, maybe ephemeral, and originally motivated by professional interest on my part, financial need on hers. Perhaps claiming Rasmata as my friend is stretching the definition too far, but I liked her immediately and instinctively. I always looked forward to seeing her, and I often think about her now.

To meet Rasmata for the first time, I had to go looking for her. I climbed onto the back of a friend's moped and headed out into *la zone non-lotie,* one of the sections on the edge of Ouagadougou colonized willy-nilly by poor people who can't afford to live inside the city. There are no roads, and we had to weave our way among the derelict walls of derelict dwellings, most of them occupied nonetheless, on footpaths that wound on indefinitely. Above all, *la zone non-lotie* has the feeling of impermanence. In fact, my first impression was that of a campground. The little homes left a life-in-miniature impression: a tiny stool instead of a chair, a log instead of a couch, pretend walls for a pretend house. This sense of impermanence was something I saw all around me in Burkina Faso, but in the *non-lotie,* I imagined the residents poised to flee the next morning, in a moment, as soon as possible. I have never visited a refugee camp, but I wonder if it might be something like this.

The women I saw in the neighborhood that first visit mostly looked like refugees—some with rotting teeth, thinning hair, scars, or other visible signs of untreated injuries or illnesses, their bodies marked by the difficulty of their lives. They stood and stared at me over the crumbling walls of their courtyards or gazed up from blankets on the ground from which they sold tiny piles of peanuts or a few vegetables. My friend went in search of Rasmata while I sat down in her courtyard and waited, thinking that each beleaguered woman that passed by, ragged and permanently dusty, must be her, but she did not come.

Eventually, we left messages with neighbors and returned to my friend's house to wait in greater comfort. So it was really Rasmata who found me, and not the other way around. She did not shuffle into my friend's courtyard but clattered up on an old bicycle, energetically and without apology. We had been later than expected, she explained, so she'd returned to her work at the market. I'd anticipated a woman like those I'd seen earlier in Rasmata's neighborhood, scarred by defeat, but I got a tourist brochure, a postcard, a cover of *National Geographic.* Rasmata looked as if she had been polished—perfect skin, perfect teeth, doe eyes, and heart-shaped face. She was also beautifully dressed, though I was too mesmerized to write anything down in my notebook other than *grand boubou,* a traditional garment composed of a long piece of loose-fitting cloth. Around her neck Rasmata had wrapped a fluorescent-orange scarf, and around her head a bright pink one. The vivid colors contrasted with the gentleness of Rasmata's features, highlighting them. I was smitten.

Rasmata, on the other hand, was not smitten with me. She was uncomfortable with my tape recorder, uncomfortable with my questions. We sat on my friend's verandah, a table and an interpreter between us. She looked down and away, smiling only rarely, demure and polite. I learned very little during my first visit: that Rasmata was born in the village of Kamboinsé, that her husband by arranged marriage was a practitioner of traditional medicine, a *tradipraticien.* Rasmata made it clear that she had not loved her husband, did not miss him, and preferred not to talk about him. "I do not speak [badly] of the dead," she said, her eyebrows raised and lips pursed in an inscrutable expression. Disgust? Some ancient and repressed anger? It was hard to know.

Hobbies and interests: Her religious faith (Islam), and chatting with neighbors and fellow market vendors.

Dreams: None. "I live day by day. I get up in the morning, and I go to sleep." Rasmata didn't dream for her children, either her ten-year-old boy, Oussini, and seven-year-old girl, Balkissa. They were going to a school for orphans at the time, but it went only through the elementary grades, and Rasmata didn't have the funds to send them to middle school. The girl might become a maid, Rasmata conceded, and the son an apprentice to a bus driver or a mechanic—if they were lucky.

Worries and concerns: None. "There is nothing I can do but pray."

In retrospect, I could have asked Rasmata many more questions than I did that afternoon. She needed whatever money I might give her in compensation for her time, so the balance of power was all on my side. But there was something about her physical presence, a certain serenity and authority, that corrected the imbalance a little, not completely, but enough. Because she was reluctant to speak, I found I could not ask. Because to request a photograph seemed suddenly importunate, I did not. At the same time, I felt I had learned something important about Rasmata. In her beauty, for example, I saw a strength of spirit, the sense that she had not given in, not allowed her skin to be touched, her body to be whittled down. In her straight back and unsmiling face, I saw her will—the intention to decide for herself.

I went back to visit Rasmata again without my tape recorder. She laughed at seeing my white face bobbing along on the paths of the *non-lotie,* laughed again to see that I wore my own *grand boubou* that day. I sat on a tiny stool under a mango tree and we chatted in the ordinary way: How are you? How is your family? If I stayed with Rasmata for more than fifteen minutes that day, I'd be surprised. I felt out of place; I literally was out of my place, having crossed social boundaries of every kind to get to the little stool where I sat. The children of Rasmata's neighborhood made it clear to me what a strange sight I was. They shadowed me, gathering to watch me over the wall of Rasmata's courtyard. "*Nassara, nassara*,"—white woman—I heard them whisper, sounding like branches brushing together in the wind.

I don't remember worrying about whether or not Rasmata was happy to see me, but I believe she was. At least she greeted me with warmth and spoke with animation to the translator who accompanied me—while looking at me the way you might look at an unattractive suitor whose surprising good qualities you have suddenly discovered. The freedom with which she smiled and laughed eased my discomfort, and I would have gone to visit Rasmata again during that summer if my stay in her country had been longer.

I did send greetings from the United States, however, and spent more time with her when I returned to Burkina Faso the following summer to continue my research. One day, I brought her to the house I'd rented in Ouagadougou, where she perched on the edge of my sofa like a bird and admired the curtains. Rasmata seemed to feel as out of place in my home as I had in hers, refusing any drink but water, barely touching the bowl of snacks I put on the table. I introduced her to my family. I know my daughter was as strange to her as I was, maybe stranger: mocha-skinned, loose curls flying in every direction, ebullient and insistent—nothing like the quiet Burkinabé children with their tight, careful braids. My Burkinabé husband she greeted with something that looked like gratitude. Though he is a chemistry professor now, my husband's mother was a market woman, and he had been a boy like Oussini, who did not know from year to year how his school fees would be paid. Rasmata relaxed in my husband's presence, relieved to find a countryman's voice and face in my strange world.

Despite her discomfort in my home, Rasmata's attitude toward me had changed by then. She greeted me with a friendliness that approached affection. It was not what she felt for her friends in the neighborhood and in the market—women she identified as the primary source of support and pleasure in her life. These friends took care of each other in all kinds of practical ways, watching each other's children, tending each other's market stalls, sharing the cost of wholesale produce, and sharing food. Still, she slapped her thighs with surprise and satisfaction when I visited, saved her children's school notebooks to show me, and held my hand when we walked together. She also introduced me to a couple of her friends—who looked at me like an interesting new species of bird—and to her children.

I learned more about Rasmata. Though she had been born in Kamboinsé, she'd grown up in the Ivory Coast with her uncle's family. The uncle had asked for her, and since "for us my child is also my brother's child," she went as a young girl to help with the housework and the new babies. "They were very nice to me," she says. "I was happy there." She only came back to Burkina Faso when her father betrothed her to a man she had never met. "You know, I had my own guy then, a teacher. When I came back and I saw this poor man my father had promised me to—he had nothing!—I knew I would suffer. So I ran back to my boyfriend, who had promised to hide me, but my family found me and brought me back."

After that she lived the life of a dutiful wife, bearing two children, though no love developed between husband and wife. They moved to the tiny cement-block hut in the *zone non-lotie* soon after they married, and there they stayed. He made extended trips to Kamboinsé when he could, often without Rasmata. Eventually, he got sick and died there—of AIDS, says our mutual friend, a nurse and public health worker—though Rasmata does not admit this. In any case, life was what she thought it would be with the *tradipraticien* she'd married—poverty-stricken. To survive, Rasmata had to fend for herself. She got fruit and vegetables from the wholesalers on credit, and she has worked in the market ever since. "I have always taken care of myself," she said proudly.

This pride and self-sufficiency were part of what drew me to Rasmata. Most of my work was in very poor communities, and every week people asked me for things that I could not give them: money, a job in the United States, someone to sponsor their children. I didn't blame anyone for asking, but sometimes I felt plucked, defoliated, the lone tree in a land of giraffes. In contrast, though she had fewer resources than anyone I met in the capital, Rasmata never asked for anything. On two occasions, in fact, she gave me gifts. For example, one day I'd taken a small sack of secondhand clothes to her market stall and then stayed for a visit. When I left, she piled my arms, and my brother-in-law's, with fruit—mangoes from the basket she'd been selling. I remember her way of giving, quick and insistent, so that if we did not accept the gift, some of the mangoes would have fallen on the ground, bruised and cracked, useless.

Also, despite the obvious and vast differences between the two of us, I identified with Rasmata in ways that I only realize now in retrospect. My husband and I have been living together for the last two years, but for the previous seven, including the first two- and-a-half years of our daughter's life, we had jobs in different states. During those seven years, I coped with a difficult pregnancy, illnesses, and working parenthood on my own. I wrote a book while teaching college full-time, chairing a small academic program, coediting a literary journal, and caring for a baby. At one point, I got so sick that I couldn't pick my daughter up, so I made a sling out of a sheet and slid her carefully from room to room along our wooden floor. Had I given up any of the work I was doing at that time, however, I might not have gotten my current job, which allows us to live together as a family. I have never had to fight a daily battle against poverty, like Rasmata does, but I have needed what was, for me, a daily courage. Like her, I am proud of my independence and what I have been able to do for my family.

My daughter and husband were with me for only a month of the three I stayed in Burkina that second summer. I was alone and lonely for most of my stay, more so because many of the companions available to me had family obligations that preoccupied them and kept them at home—domestic, domesticated. The tastes and opinions of these women seemed to mirror their husbands' or mine. Rasmata, on the other hand, had definite perspectives that she was afraid neither to withhold nor to communicate: She did not love her husband; she did not enjoy being interviewed. Even though we never discussed weighty matters beyond Rasmata's life story and the bits of my own life that she asked me about, I felt I had company in her presence. Anything she said or did and the expressions on her face were not meant to please someone else, but were dipped from the well of her own being and experience.

I have had life-changing friendships, intense relationships that bordered on or crossed into the erotic. I have had the sort of friendship in which I could talk about anything, in which I felt completely known and completely at home. Rasmata and I know each other only partially, two-dimensionally. Nevertheless, I think about her often and talk about her to my American friends now that I am at home. In fact, after hearing Rasmata's story, my smart friend Martha encouraged me to start a fund to build Rasmata a house, someplace permanent on a lot of her own. Martha helped me feel less queasy about fund-raising, and then she contributed—it was her Christmas present to her parents, and her parents' Christmas present to her. This little fund makes me happy: It makes me feel more deeply connected to Rasmata and to Martha. I also feel as though I am a link between these two women, perhaps part of a longer chain connecting Rasmata, Martha, the women friends who sustain Rasmata, and me—connecting strong women across all kinds of circumstances.

I imagine that many of these connections are fairly mundane: How are you? I am fine. How are your children? They are fine. Whether or not I succeed in building Rasmata's house, my relationship with her will probably stay on this level, too, because we don't share a language or a way of life. But I think I am right to value all the gifts of friendship, the ordinary and extraordinary. My friendship with Rasmata made my life in her country better, and it helps me keep the world of the *non-lotie* in mind now—a world so different and distant from my own that it would be easy for me to forget.

When I left Burkina Faso for the second time, I went to the market to say goodbye to my friend. For a present, I took her a little cash and a dress I didn't need. Rasmata gave me peanuts, which she had been selling out of a tattered basket. She stuffed the peanuts by the handful into a black plastic bag, pushed them down so the shape of the nuts showed through the plastic. When she was done, her basket was almost empty.

Acknowledgments

This book was made possible by all the women who contributed their stories of friendship—those you'll find in these pages and those I was unable to include. Thank you for your generosity, willingness, and patience.

I couldn't help but reflect on my own friendships as I edited this collection. If I thought I could do them justice, I would write chapters celebrating each of these companions and confidants who, whether in turn or in overlap, saw me through safely from childhood to young adulthood and beyond: Mara Schwartz, Therese Peffer, Kim Hammer, Michelle Denny, Marlene Bergo, Katie Avenson, Nikki Mann, Lisa Nagel, Lorraine Farrington-Bone, Liz Bailey, Shauna Swartz, Chris Hudson, Linda Allen, and Suzanne Stanford. I am also lucky to have many cherished male friends. I would especially like to thank Jef Davis, Richard Siebert, Peter Koch, Timothy Pearson, Philip Hopkins, Jed Caesar, and Robert Toren for their support and unstinting faith in me.

Thanks to Andi Zeisler for offering a ready, steady voice of reason, Lisa Jervis and Ayun Halliday for their veterans' guidance, and Leslie Miller, my astute editor at Seal Press, for thinking this was a good idea and urging me on. Ali and Carolyn—thanks for reminding me how exciting it can be to start all over again, making new friends in a new town.

And thanks most of all to my lovely husband, Iain Mann.

About the Contributors

Sara Bir's writing has appeared in a variety of publications, including *Saveur, ReadyMade, PekoPeko,* and the *North Bay Bohemian.* She works at a chocolate factory in Berkeley, California.

Ariel Bordeaux is a cartoonist and illustrator living in Rhode Island. She has written and drawn a graphic novella and several mini-comics, and has contributed to such publications as *Bust, Dirty Stories, Hate, Nickelodeon, The Stranger,* and *True Porn.* Currently, she is working on a serialized comic book called *Raisin Pie,* which she shares authorship of with her husband, Rick Altergott. More of her work may be seen at www.arielbordeaux.com.

Kathleen Collins is a writer and researcher living in New York City. She has written several nonfiction children's books, encyclopedia entries on media history, and reviews and essays for *Bitch* and *PekoPeko.*

Juliet Eastland writes and plays piano in New York City. She composed and played the music for *Andromania: Men/Sex/Madness* at HERE Theater. Her writing has appeared in *Bitch* magazine, indiebride.com, knotmag.com, and several essay anthologies.

Ellen Forney's work has appeared in many publications including *LA Weekly, BUST, Nickelodeon,* and *The Stranger.* Her book of autobiographical comic strips, *Monkey Food: The Complete "I Was Seven in '75" Collection* (Fantagraphics Books) was nominated for several national comics awards. She has been teaching courses on comics at Cornish College of the Arts since 2002. More of her work is at www.ellenforney.com.

Myriam Gurba's nonfiction has appeared in a variety of magazines, including *Girlfriends* and *Punk Planet,* while her fiction has appeared in various anthologies and magazines. She lives in California and is a high school teacher.

Ayun Halliday is the sole staff member of the quarterly zine *The East Village Inky* and is the author of *The Big Rumpus: A Mother's Tale from the Trenches* and *No Touch Monkey! and Other Travel Lessons Learned Too Late.* She is *BUST's* Mother Superior columnist and also contributes to National Public Radio, *Hip Mama*, and more anthologies than you can shake a stick at without dangling a participle. She lives in Brooklyn, where she's hard at work on her next book, *Job Hopper.*

Marisa Handler (marisa_handler@hotmail.com) is a poet, activist, writer, and musician living in San Francisco. Her work has appeared in such publications as Salon.com, *Bitch,* the *San Francisco Chronicle,* the *Bay Guardian,* and *Tikkun,* as well as in anthologies and Indymedia. Marisa is very active in Direct Action to Stop the War as well as the Bay Area chapter of United for Peace and Justice.

Marrit Ingman is a freelance essayist and cultural critic whose work has appeared in the *Austin Chronicle, Isthmus, Coast Weekly,* and *Mamalicious.* She has taught nonfiction writing at Boston University and Springfield College and specializes in film criticism. She is a contributing reviewer for the *Chronicle* and teaches after-school courses on the cinema at Fulmore Middle School. She also works as a filmmaker and is currently developing a self-produced documentary on alternative parenting in the United States. She lives in Austin, Texas, with her family.

Molly Kiely is an artist and cartoonist who recently escaped the San Francisco Bay area for a three-acre ranchette northwest of Tucson, Arizona. She'll take turkeys gobbling at 3 A.M. over car alarms any day. She has written and drawn over a dozen comics and two graphic novels. These and other works can be seen at mollykiely.com.

Shira Kozak grew up in Reading, Pennsylvania. She loves both writing and reading romance novels, toy collecting, and attempting to grow a garden. She is currently an operations officer for a government contractor in Arizona. Ms. Kozak lives with her military husband, Roy, son Christopher, and an overly friendly Labrador retriever named Licorice. She is currently hard at work on her novel "Trinity."

Alison Krupnick lives in Seattle with her husband and two young daughters. Her work has appeared in *Fugue* and *Brain, Child: The Magazine for Thinking Mothers,* and is forthcoming in *Contemporary Women in Creative Pursuit: Motherhood Poetry Anthology 2003* (Purple Canary Press). She is currently at work on a collection of essays entitled "Ruminations from the Minivan."

Jacqueline Lalley grew up in Madison, Wisconsin, and has lived in Chicago for the past ten years. Her poetry has appeared in *Harvard Review, Bridge, Nebraska Review, Court Green,* and other places, and her nonfiction has been published—if not widely, then deeply. She has an undergraduate degree in women's studies from Mt. Holyoke College and an MFA in poetry. To pay the bills, she works as a communications and publishing consultant for nonprofit organizations. She is currently organizing the Independent Press Association of Chicago.

Jennifer Maher teaches in the gender studies department at Indiana University at Bloomington. She is a frequent contributer to *Bitch* and estimates that she has read *Harriet the Spy* over twenty times.

L. A. Miller is the editor of *Women Who Eat: A New Generation on the Glory of Food*, and has also published essays in *Bitch* magazine and in numerous anthologies. She is currently at work on a book about Las Vegas weddings. She lives in Seattle.

Jennifer D. Munro's credits include a story (published under a pseudonym) in the Seal Press anthology *Shameless: Women's Intimate Erotica.* She has also been published in *Calyx; Kalliope; Room of One's Own; They Lied! True Tales of Pregnancy, Childbirth, & Breastfeeding; Threads That Bind; Knitting Stories; Best Women's Erotica 2003; Best American Erotica 2004; Slow Trains, Clean Sheets,* and others. She has been a Hedgebrook resident, an Artist Trust grant recipient, and winner of the Seattle Writers Association essay contest.

Sophie Radice lives in North London with her husband and two children, a son who is 13 and a daughter who is 9. She writes on a regular basis for UK newspapers the *Observer* and the *Guardian.* She is currently writing a novel.

Joshunda Sanders is a bookworm who lives in Oakland, California, with her two cats, James and Zora, and makes home anywhere she finds it. She has worked as a journalist and writer for several years and has contributed to *Vibe, Africana.com, The Houston Chronicle, The Seattle Post-Intelligencer,* and many other publications. She is writing a memoir about the Bronx. She's currently a features writer for the *San Francisco Chronicle.*

Ariel Schrag is the author of the autobiographical comic books *Awkward, Definition, Potential,* and *Likewise* (Slave Labor), which chronicle her four years at Berkeley High School. Each book was written and drawn during the summer after the year it covers. Current projects include writing the screen adaptation of *Potential* for Killer Films; inking *Likewise,* which is being published in an eight-issue series; and putting together a collection of short stories about her college years. She may be contacted at arielschrag@hotmail.com.

8730

Mara Schwartz is a writer and music industry executive who lives in Silver Lake, California. Her writing has appeared in the *Los Angeles Times, LA Weekly, Seventeen,* and many other publications.

Lauren Bower Smith is an essayist, a poet, and a professor of women's studies who lives and works in Whitewater, Wisconsin. With co-writer and friend Jessie Grearson, she has published two books on intercultural families, *Swaying* and *Love in a Global Village* (University of Iowa Press). Her current solo project is a collection of essays, "A West African AIDS Quilt," describing the lives and struggles of West Africans touched by the AIDS epidemic.

Andi Zeisler is a writer, editor, and illustrator. She is the co-founder and editorial director of *Bitch: Feminist Response to Pop Culture,* and her writing has also appeared in *Ms., Mother Jones, BUST, PekoPeko,* and the *Women's Review of Books.* She lives in Oakland, California, with her husband and dog, and is currently at work on a book about pessimism.

About the Editor

Karen Eng is a freelance writer and editor who has worked in the magazine industry since 1991. She has published a wide range of articles, mainly about independent arts and culture, in a variety of publications, among them *Bitch: Feminist Response to Pop Culture*. Her essays are included in the Seal Press anthologies *Women Who Eat* and *Young Wives' Tales*. In 2002, she received a George Washington Williams journalism fellowship sponsored by the Independent Press Association. In her spare time, she enjoys letterpress, photography, producing *PekoPeko: a zine about food,* and dreaming up more indie-publishing schemes than she—or her friends—can handle.

Selected Titles from Seal Press

Inappropriate Random: Stories on Sex and Love edited by Amy Prior. $13.95, 1-58005-099-9. Established and emerging American and British women writers take a hard look at love, exposing its flaws with unflinching, often hilarious, candor.

Women Who Eat: A New Generation on the Glory of Food edited by Leslie Miller. $15.95, 1-58005-092-1. More than just great food writing, this long-overdue rebuttal to the notion that all women are on a diet celebrates food with grace, wit, and gusto.

Chelsea Whistle by Michelle Tea. $14.95, 1-58005-073-5. In this gritty, confessional memoir, Michelle Tea takes the reader back to the city of her childhood: Chelsea, Massachusetts—Boston's ugly, scrappy little sister and a place where time and hope are spent on things not getting any worse.

Atlas of the Human Heart by Ariel Gore. $14.95, 1-58005-088-3. Ariel Gore spins the spirited story of a vulnerable drifter who takes refuge in the fate and the shadowy recesses of a string of glittering, broken relationships.

The Big Rumpus: A Mother's Tales from the Trenches by Ayun Halliday. $15.95, 1-58005-071-9. Creator of the wildly popular *East Village Inky,* Halliday describes the quirks and everyday travails of a young urban family, warts and all.

Cunt: A Declaration of Independence by Inga Muscio. $14.95, 1-58005-075-1. An ancient title of respect for women, "cunt" long ago veered off the path of honor and now careens toward the heart of every woman as an expletive. Muscio traces this winding road, giving women both the motivation and the tools to claim "cunt" as a positive and powerful force in the lives of all women.

Seal Press publishes many books of fiction and nonfiction by women writers. Please visit our website at **www.sealpress.com.**